WA
WITH
THE
WEARY

LIFE-CHANGING LESSONS IN HEALTHCARE

DR M. R. RAJAGOPAL

ALEPH

ALEPH

ALEPH BOOK COMPANY
An independent publishing firm
promoted by *Rupa Publications India*

Published in India in 2022
by Aleph Book Company
7/16 Ansari Road, Daryaganj
New Delhi 110 002

First published as *Walk with the Weary: Lessons in humanity in health care* by Notion Press in 2022.

Copyright © M. R. Rajagopal 2022.

All rights reserved.

The author has asserted his moral rights.

The views and opinions expressed in this book are those of the author and the facts are as reported by him, which have been verified to the extent possible, and the publisher is not in any way liable for the same.

The publisher has used its best endeavours to ensure that URLs for external websites referred to in this book are correct and active at the time of going to press. However, the publisher has no responsibility for the websites and can make no guarantee that a site will remain live or that the content is or will remain appropriate.

No part of this publication may be reproduced, transmitted, or stored in a retrieval system, in any form or by any means, without permission in writing from Aleph Book Company.

ISBN: 978-93-93852-44-1

1 3 5 7 9 10 8 6 4 2

Printed in India.

This book is sold subject to the condition that it shall not, by way of trade or otherwise, be lent, resold, hired out, or otherwise circulated without the publisher's prior consent in any form of binding or cover other than that in which it is published.

WALK WITH THE WEARY

CONTENTS

Foreword   ix
Preface   xiii

EARLY DAYS

1. Pain, Grace, and Resilience   3
2. The First Death   6
3. Tryst with Mahatma Gandhi   10
4. First Day in Medical College   15
5. Screams That Stayed with Me   21
6. The Good and the Bad   24

THE MAKING OF AN ANAESTHESIOLOGIST

7. Falling in Love   35
8. Doctors Only See the Disease   43
9. Morris, the Harbinger of Light   46
10. Awakening to Pain   51
11. The Generous Listener   56
12. Are There Any Patients for Nerve Blocks?   60

DISCOVERING PALLIATIVE CARE

13. Letting Him Go Gently into the Night   67
14. My First Affair with Community Engagement   72

15. The Group of Seven: Pain and Palliative Care Society	77
16. My UK Sojourn	80
17. Shaping a New Paradigm	83
18. On the Oral Morphine Trail	89
19. Navigating Indian Bureaucracy	94

DEPTHS OF SUFFERING; HEIGHTS OF RELIEF

20. Children Need Answers	101
21. Adieu, in Anger	107
22. Hope Lost; Hope Regained	110
23. A Box of Treasures	114
24. Pain That Fills Life	117
25. Many Fall between the Cracks	121

NEW BEGINNING; MORE LEARNINGS

26. Going Home	129
27. A Scar on a Neck	135
28. Kerala Palliative Care Policy	140
29. Pain Misunderstood World Over	143
30. A Life Lesson	151
31. Conversations on Sex	156

LIVES SHARED

32. Suffering Matters	161
33. Anxiety and Disquiet	166

34. Letting Go	171
35. Glow in the Dark	178
36. No One Should Die Alone	183
37. Stripped of All Rights	186
38. Imprisoned in an Emotional Fortress	192

LOVE, CONNECTIONS, DIGNITY

39. Connections	199
40. What Makes God Happy?	206
41. Faith and Religion	211
42. Care Is Not a One-way Street	216
43. Palliative Care Is for All Illness-Related Suffering	221
44. Engage, or Assist the Harm	225
45. Celebrating Life; Celebrating Death	230

Epilogue	234
Acknowledgements	237
Closing	239

FOREWORD

Dr M. R. Rajagopal, whom I am fortunate to count as a constituent, is one of a handful of physicians who can truly be described as having permanently changed the face of Indian healthcare. The founder-chairman of Pallium India, a non-governmental organization, he has been the foremost supporter and propagator of palliative care in India. On the occasion of the publication of his book *Walk with the Weary*, I am delighted to offer these words of tribute.

Walk with the Weary is a fascinating book. From heartbreaking stories of family tragedy, to an inspiring defence of palliative care and pain relief, it details Dr Rajagopal's commitment to providing compassionate care for those suffering from chronic pain. His own journey, the support of his wife, and the many sacrifices he had to undertake, all speak to his visionary selflessness in pursuing his dream.

Above all, the impression one gets from Dr Rajagopal is his ceaseless dedication to preserving the dignity of his patients. Pain ultimately takes away one's dignity. Therefore, if you can ease pain you are actually strengthening the dignity of a sufferer, and contributing a great deal to easing the memories left behind in the hearts and minds and souls of the survivors and the families. Dr Rajagopal's work and writing makes clear that it is truly an embodiment of that famous expression: 'to cure sometimes, to relieve often, to comfort always'.

It must be said that where a doctor cannot add years to a patient's life at least he (or she) can add life to a patient's years—or months, or weeks—that may remain. They all know they have no hope and yes, they've all been told. And in many cases, of course, one would like them to have their last days at home in dignity. But where some medical intervention is required, it is essential to be able to give them attention and palliative care. And then the human impulse comes in: if people have to die—if there is nothing beyond a point that we can do to prevent or delay that moment of grief—at least we can ensure that they do not die in unnecessary pain.

That is where the importance of palliative care comes in: easing pain, enhancing dignity, trying to ease the memories of the survivors. All of these reasons are really what you are accomplishing with your efforts in palliative care. People all want to live a good life but they don't often remember how important it is that we also have a good death. And while death is inevitable, a painful, undignified, sad death is not necessary.

It is this mission to which Dr Rajagopal has dedicated his life. I am humbled by the grace and humanity that Dr Rajagopal and his fellow physicians, not to mention their families and the legions of medical staff who work under them, display every day in their remarkably challenging profession, one which commands—and receives—total dedication. They are the pride of Kerala and of India.

I was pleased to launch an early, privately published edition of this short memoir. I am delighted now that *Walk with the Weary* has found a major professional publisher in Aleph, and it is my hope that this book creates greater awareness of the incredible work that Dr Rajagopal has done. I wish him, and his work, all the very best.

—Shashi Tharoor

PREFACE

Are you afraid of death?

You are not? Good for you. If you can continue to maintain that frame of mind, when the time comes, you might be able to say with a smile: 'I am ready.'

On the other hand, if you are a bit afraid, you are in good company. The vast majority of human beings are afraid of the unknown, including death, the inevitable consequence of life.

You may escape for the time being by not thinking about it. But the day will come when you cannot help but think about it.

If you are the kind of person who says, 'I am not afraid of death but...' you are possibly not afraid of death itself, but of the process of dying.

Often, we hold back such fears. What is it like to die? Will it be painful? And what lies beyond?

Lessons learned from people living with various diseases can help one understand death far more than you would imagine. My palliative care journey amidst pain, suffering, and relief has also offered many life-changing experiences. You might find them reassuring, uplifting, or, at times, even empowering.

The stories I share here* have enriched my life and taught me many valuable lessons, which have the ability to prepare you to some day face the illness or even death of someone else, or your own. And, perhaps, it will empower you to not only face the situation, but also be able to help the person. You may then be able to resist the temptation to turn away from it all. You may have the equanimity to be there with the person in pain or approaching death, holding his or her hand, leaning in with a caring touch, and when the time is up, to let go with all the tenderness and love you hold within you.

---

*Some names have been changed to maintain anonymity.

EARLY DAYS

Education is that which remains, if one has forgotten everything he learnt in school.

—Albert Einstein[*]

---

[*]Albert Einstein, 'On Education', available at <www.andrew.cmu.edu/user/sobla/teaching/On_Education_Einstein.pdf>.

ONE

PAIN, GRACE, AND RESILIENCE

One of my earliest pleasant memories is of a small brook that would appear with the first rain and make its way through the middle of the two-acre farm where I lived with Ammachi, my grandmother, and Appooppan, my grandfather.

Ammachi, Appooppan, and the day-help Muthu completed my otherwise lonely world during those few years.

My father had always wanted a daughter and my birth as a third boy was a big disappointment to him, or so was said in those days. When my younger sister was born, I was sent away, at the age of three, to live with my grandparents in another village a few miles away.

It was a poor neighbourhood. The children living in tiny huts around our farm belonged to 'lower' castes and, as the caste system was deeply entrenched in the psyche of the older generation, I was not allowed to play with them.

Ammachi would sit with me by the stream and help me build tiny dams. She played with me when I waded into the water. She made paper boats for me that could sail in the shallow lakes I created, while the stream merrily gurgled its way down, winding across the farm to join a small pond, which offered itself to the villagers to bathe in.

I loved the clear springs that appeared in the slopes during monsoon and sang their way towards the stream. But memories of the stream also bring in the memory of my first encounter with serious pain.

Appooppan had taken me up a slope to our farm, where he had some spading work to do. The spot was a little away from our home. I sat there watching him prepare the ground for planting.

All of a sudden, he crumpled and fell over. A severe pain in his back twisted his body sideways, rendering him unable to move for what seemed like a long time. I was too small, I suppose, to be sent to get help. He could have screamed, and someone might have heard him and come to help. But he was not the screaming type. He was the hardy kind, having gone through a very tough life as an orphan, with only an elder brother to bring him up. The self-made part of him was his true self.

He eventually managed to pull himself up to a cross-legged sitting position. Then, using his hands, he moved down the slope, painfully and very slowly. That's when my stream stumped him. He sat there, brooding, still not asking me to help in any way. I remember fear and helplessness filling me.

Thankfully, Ammachi saw us a while later. She came running and helped him negotiate the stream. The steep flight of steps to the house caused much agony to both of them.

Gabrivaidyan, the village physician, came with his indigenous medicines and Appooppan was up and about in a few days.

My grandfather was a master of stoic acceptance, and I admired it. That day he taught me to accept with grace what I could not change.

Looking back, I see a pattern in many stories of suffering I witnessed as a doctor. Most people are initially reluctant to ask for help. Then, with great hesitation, they ask someone who is not very sensitive and would not oblige. The helplessness then turns to anger, and reproach, 'Why on earth did I ask him? I should have known that no one cares.'

This is clearly not true. Many people with serious health issues have said so. A calamity serves as a sieve, to sort out our true friends from the uncaring ones. Just when some 'close' friends quietly vanish from the scene of your misfortune, others appear and support you.

For instance, take the story of Ashla Rani. Ashla says that after having lived with quadriplegia for four years, it was a moment of epiphany when she was told that receiving care and support were her rights and not mere charity. But she had no power to claim her right if someone did not acknowledge it. Knowing this ineffable truth gave her the courage to ask for what was duly hers.

Ashla joined Pallium India as a volunteer. She chipped in to help as my executive assistant, and went on to counsel people with disabilities.

Ashla is now a trustee of Pallium India.

Any cultured society has a responsibility to lend a hand to those who need it. Not everyone accepts that responsibility. But many do.

Over the years, I have learnt from many patients and their families that I should not be afraid to ask for help. I should learn to accept rejection with equanimity, and support with gratitude.

TWO

THE FIRST DEATH

One day, I was woken up in the middle of the night, as it often happens when a tragedy unfolds in a family. An uncle had died. Too groggy to walk, I was carried in the arms of my tiny Ammachi for several miles all the way to the house. I was puny, but I was a growing child, and it must have been tiring for my frail Ammachi to carry me all the way. Appooppan walked ahead; clearly, carrying a child was the woman's duty.

I woke up to the sound of wailing women in my uncle's home. The closest family members were weeping and were being propped up by several helping hands. Young men from the neighbourhood had been dispatched to inform relatives and neighbours about the death.

It took several hours for the entire extended family to arrive. Some travelled from far off villages to reach the house. One family narrated to whoever cared to listen how they had missed the only bus from their village and were compelled to travel in a bullock cart for some distance before walking the rest of the way.

The arrival of each family member stirred up some drama. Some relatives were meeting after months or even years. Children were excitedly rushing around, confused but not disturbed by the gloomy backdrop.

At the centre of it all was the funeral pyre—the reason why we were all there. We would all be inevitably drawn to it.

A few men were digging a pit several feet deep in the yard, while some others were felling a mango tree for wood to be used for the cremation. The chopped logs were arranged at the bottom of the pit over which several layers of coconut husks were arranged and kept ready for the body.

The body was bathed under the leadership of the village barber, who was to oversee the funeral rites as per custom. The deceased was carried to the funeral pit and laid on the bed of husks with his head to the south; the direction ruled by Yama, the god of death. This would be the first time my uncle would be lying down in this position. In his lifetime, he would not have slept with his head southward as it was inauspicious to do so.

The younger relatives gently dropped grains of raw rice into the mouth of my uncle to symbolize the offering of a last meal. Each of us, both adults and children, circled his body thrice in a slow-moving queue, and prayed. Wailing women were supported by relatives. The heartbroken ones, who wanted to linger around the body, were gently nudged forward.

My uncle did not have a son. His brother's son, playing the part, carried an earthen pot filled with water on his head as he circled the body. Once he reached the feet, an elder sharply cracked the pot with a heavy knife, allowing the water to flow out, as he went around the pyre.

The barber piled more husks over the body and added another layer of logs. The nephew lit the pile with a torch, making the pyre crackle and smoke. Most people in the crowd walked away. A few lingered to hold vigil.

In the evenings during the period of mourning, Ammachi took me to my parents' house which was nearby, where my two brothers and sister lived. Oh, yes, my own home for me was where I lived with my Ammachi and Appooppan—the lonely place. My parents' place was cheery in comparison. I could play with Vikramanchettan, my elder brother, who was three years older than me. My younger sister, Sudha, was pretty but bossy, and made me cry sometimes. Yet, it was heaven. I enjoyed the thrill death had brought into my life, even if briefly.

Every morning, we were back in the house of mourning, which would be overflowing with relatives. Harihara Annan, my elder brother's friend, who seemed to be the know-all in our circles, was a crowd puller. He gathered all the children around him and told stories. He described heaven and hell in graphic detail. The younger children, like me, believed his every word, including what hell looked like. The picture of ordeal in hell he painted was so scary that I instantly vowed never to sin in my life.

When hungry, we children would run to the kitchen in uncle's house for a simple meal of rice gruel, lentils, or coconut chutney. The family's many relatives had taken over the kitchen, cooking and gently persuading the family members to eat. According to custom, close relatives took care of the kitchen expenses for the next sixteen days, allowing the anguished family to grieve. As the days passed, the wailings lessened and then stopped altogether. Some took longer to let go. The sadder ones were gently persuaded to take a bath, to look after their children, and to steadily return to their daily life.

On the fifth day, there was the sanchayanam ceremony. The barber dug up the funeral pit and collected several pieces of bone, which he put into a small urn wrapped with a red silk scarf. The urn was placed in the front of the house. Everyone took turns to pray. We were not praying for the dead man any longer. We were praying to him. He was now a soul in the spiritual realm and his blessings were sacred.

Looking back, I feel the extended family system and the rituals associated with death had helped the bereaved family to cope.

At that time, I didn't realize that my uncle's death had taught me a great lesson in life. Quite involuntarily, I had learnt to accept death as a natural part of life.

Modern families tend to shield children from inconveniences such as death. I remember a former colleague's grandson being sent away from his dying father's bedside to an uncle's house so he could prepare for his high school examination. The boy was denied his last hug, and the last tears he would shed for his father. He was denied the time to grieve and with that a chance for healing. The scars would remain for a very long time.

THREE

TRYST WITH MAHATMA GANDHI

I was around ten years old when I first read Mahatma Gandhi's autobiography *The Story of My Experiments with Truth*. It is odd how circumstances can influence your life. If I had been a little more normal, I may not have had time to delve into Mahatma Gandhi's life at that age.

I was lonely at school. All my classmates were three years older than me. I had been tutored at home from the age of three by Appooppan, a retired schoolmaster. I joined formal schooling only in the fourth grade, at the early age of six. Rather than being celebrated as a child prodigy, the early start had made me a total misfit. Thankfully, Appooppan had inculcated the habit of reading in me, which helped me overcome some of my loneliness. I was never physically alone. My doting grandmother was always quick to give me a hug or a snack whenever I appeared sad. And though remote and non-communicative, I knew my grandfather was very fond of me.

Harichettan, my eldest brother, was six years older than me and belonged to another generation and another zone. My domineering sister Sudha, whom I adored, lived far away with my parents. When I was six, my second brother Vikramanchettan, came into my world, or rather we moved into his.

My parents had to move to a distant city after my father got promoted to the post of a higher level magistrate; they only took the eldest and youngest among their children with them. Perhaps it was too expensive to take all of us along. We were by no means rich—practically no one in our village was in those days. So, it was now Vikramanchettan and I who lived with our grandparents, at Muttacaud, in my parents' old home.

Vikramanchettan was very protective of me and watched over me like a hawk. He became my guide, guardian, and philosopher in every sense. Many decades later, he confessed that I was a constant source of anxiety for him in those days. He felt that I was not capable of handling the world around me.

Parallel to changes happening in my life, India was going through an exciting period after breaking free from colonial rule. There was hope in the air. Poverty was lower than before and stories of the poor dying in droves from famine seemed to be behind us. The poor were being offered employment at greater rates, and their children had more food to eat. Though my father belonged to a family of landowners, I had been told that they did not have enough to eat when they were children. We were fortunate to not grow up with hunger as a companion.

During weekends and on vacations my brother would disappear to play with his peers. Of course, I had no entry into those exalted circles. I found refuge in my books. I was lucky that the library movement had picked up pace all over the country during that period. Lending libraries had opened in most villages and we had one too. The benevolent Bhagavan maman (that was his nickname, God uncle) was the librarian.

I never got to know his real name. He was paid a meagre allowance for being the librarian, but seemed happy to be among books. A two-mile walk to the library became my daily routine during the summer vacations. I would borrow a book I found interesting and start reading it even as I walked back home. I suppose my love for walking also has its roots somewhere here.

The library rules allowed only one book at a time. One day the book I borrowed was so short that I finished reading it even before I got home. I stopped in my tracks, worried. What would I read for the rest of the day? I walked back to Bhagavan maman to exchange the book for another. With a smile that lit up his withered face, he made a special rule for me—I could borrow four books a day.

One of the books that I took home that day was the Malayalam translation of *The Story of My Experiments with Truth*.

I was profoundly inspired by Gandhi's writings. What particularly appealed to me was his courage and integrity. He once called off a successful agitation after some of his followers turned violent and torched a police station killing twenty-two policemen, which violated his principle of non-violence. His followers, including Jawaharlal Nehru, pleaded with him not to abandon the agitation. But he did not budge. He believed that if we could kill, we were not ready to govern ourselves. I admired the strength of his conviction. It made a deep impression on my young mind.

Perhaps, Gandhi's courage appealed to me so much because I was a timid child, who longed to be brave. If I was falsely accused of something in the school, I didn't have the courage to speak in my own defence. I would look pleadingly at Vikramanchettan if he was around. If he wasn't, I would quietly scoot away, ashamed of my cowardice. I wanted a bit of the Gandhian courage.

But I didn't realize how much Gandhi had influenced me until I joined a yoga course a few decades later. The instructor asked us to close our eyes and focus on a favourite deity or a guru. I closed my eyes and Gandhi's image sprung up unbidden in my mind.

I wonder what Gandhi would have done for this country if he had not been killed at the age of seventy-eight, a year after Indian independence. I feel sad that most freedom fighters did not join him when he toured one troubled city after another trying to bring peace even as religious fanatics were killing following the partition of India and Pakistan.

Many decades after his death, Gandhi still lives in the hearts and minds of a lot of people. Some put him on a pedestal, but I feel that's a convenient way to tell ourselves that he was a saint and we, mere mortals, cannot aspire to the values he embodied.

I was just one of the millions whom Gandhi influenced. He shaped my palliative care work and my life, not by his words, but through his life. He taught me not to turn away when something needed to be done and I had the power to try. He taught me that it was acceptable to fail; but unacceptable not to try. I admired his tenacity of purpose, how he clung on to the idea of freedom for India and did not let go of it.

I remember his words when I have to walk unknown paths. 'Whenever you are in doubt, or when the self becomes too much with you, apply the following test: recall the face of the poorest and the weakest man [woman] whom you may have seen, and ask yourself, if the step you contemplate is going to be of any use to him [her]. Will he [she] gain anything by it? Will it restore him [her] to a control over his [her] own life and destiny?"

---

*As quoted in Pyarelal, *Mahatma Gandhi: The Last Phase*, Vol. II, Ahmedabad: Navajivan Publishing House, 1958.

FOUR

FIRST DAY IN MEDICAL COLLEGE

It was the September of 1965. At the age of seventeen, I got admission to the Trivandrum Medical College in Kerala. I was not really keen to study medicine and would have preferred English literature. But I was offered a seat at the medical college based on my marks. It was the Holy Grail. My father said 'Go', and I went.

I found that despite my reading, I had not imbibed much of Gandhi's courage. I was still scared. I already had a degree in zoology. Did a Bachelor of Science have any right to tremble in fear? I tried to contain my anxiety, but failed miserably. I had to walk into that strange world alone. I longed for Vikramanchettan to walk by my side.

The fact that a son from our family was joining a medical college was quite an event at home. It was the first time that anyone from my village had secured a seat in a medical college. And this called for dramatic sartorial changes; the dhoti had to give way to long trousers for the first time. White cotton cloth was purchased from Binny Showroom and handed over to a veteran tailor. I was blissfully unaware that his tailoring experience was probably limited to stitching pillowcases. However, he bravely rose to the occasion. One day before the college opened, I got my fancy new attire. It looked good but there was one major problem—it was too large. My trousers seemed to keep a respectful two-inch distance from me.

You could not buy leather belts in my village. Coir, yes. Twine, maybe. Not many people wore trousers in the village. There was no reason for any store to stock leather belts. There was nothing to do but to wait until morning to buy one when I got to the city.

I don't know how my trousers stayed up the next morning. Keeping a hand in one of the pockets helped, but mostly it was willpower. My firm single-minded objective that morning was to get to the town and buy a belt.

However, an unexpected misfortune struck while I was en route to the town. A girl from my neighbouring village had also secured a seat in the medical college. She was also creating history in her village for being the first to join medicine. I am not implying that I considered it a misfortune to meet girls. It was just that I would have preferred to have a closer contact with my trousers when I met them. She was obviously as nervous as I was to attend college for the first time and was glad to have company. She stuck to me like a limpet.

We got to East Fort—the transit bus station. It was only 6.30 a.m. and we were very early. We had taken the first bus because it was the only one that would get us from our village to the college on time.

'I have something to do. I shall be back in a few minutes,' I told my new friend and walked away briskly. I was careful to retain contact with my trousers. No stores were open at that early hour. My anxiety mounted with each step. Eventually, I found a shop that was open and was stocking the merchandise I required.

First Day in Medical College 17

The belt restored my confidence. I felt like a new man, and quickly walked back to East Fort. It was 7.30 a.m. The girl gave me an annoyed look, but only for a second. She looked at my belt and hid a smile. We boarded a bus to the college.

Two groups of seniors zeroed in on us just as we entered the campus, ragging, of course. The 'lucky' gang got the girl, leaving the rather disappointed second bunch to toy with me. They decided to make the best use of what was available, meaning me.

The leader of the gang was a very kind person. He gave me a lot of advice on how to respect my alma mater and instructed me to start showing my respect by saluting every single window of the medical college hospital. I had to do that standing in the middle of the road. A lot of amused spectators watched the show and laughed as they passed by. Some even stopped by to watch.

Most of that day went by in a blur. I walked in a daze through college corridors and sat in classrooms not registering much of what was going on. But there is one thing that I remember clearly—my first lecture in physiology.

I watched as two young tutors, both doctors, came in and marked our attendance, while the professor stood watching benevolently. This business of marking attendance was quite a ritual. The tutors took turns calling out our names, mostly mispronounced and resulting in some funny errors; they had been typed up by an obviously busy typist (or one with a warped sense of humour). They called out 'ParlinNorlin' and waited for the surprised murmurs to subside, when a confused and embarrassed Pearline Nalini stood up to point out that she may be the ParlinNorlin they were looking for. The tutors seemed to almost give up trying to call out

Authman Saleh Authman, our classmate from Lebanon, and Sivagnanasegaran, a student from Malaysia. I could see why the professor would not want to do the roll call. What use were the young tutors, if not to do such awkward chores?

But even the most entertaining shows have to come to an end. As it turned out, the most exciting and fun part of that hour was over. The professor took the stage for the lecture. To this day, what she talked about remains a deep mystery to me. I could only figure out that the plot revolved around two central characters with musical names—chronaxie and rheobase. Those two characters may have been meaningful to researchers of tissue irritability, as I know now, but I had no clue why they were important during the first lecture of my medical education.

Looking back now, I can see what happened. The stress of the beltless trousers had weakened my spirit, the endless task of 'respectation' (yes, I coined that word) of the hospital windows had taxed my body and spirit. No existing word would describe what I had to do that day wrapped in endless shame and self-loathing. I was in a state of near-total exhaustion. I could not have absorbed any information on chronaxie or rheobase. I gave up.

The whole episode seems funny to me when I look back, and I can even recall the day with a smile now. But there are some sad elements in this narrative that trouble me. Ragging still goes on in medical colleges. There was this tragic story in 2009 where a young student had succumbed to injuries sustained during ragging.[*] There are cases of suicides

---

[*]Naresh K. Sharma and Anand Bodh, 'Medical student killed in ragging', *Times of India*, 10 March 2009.

triggered by ragging reported periodically from all over the country. To me, ragging is simply an abuse of power.

I survived saluting what seemed like hundreds of windows. I was the object of ridicule for my seniors. I had felt embarrassed that patients and passers-by had witnessed my torture. However, I got off lightly. Many of my classmates, who were residents of the medical college hostel, were stripped naked, I came to know later. Some of them were made to masturbate in front of their tormentors. Girls were verbally abused by the male seniors. Our society, by being mere witnesses, conveyed the message that it approved of this manner of initiation into the medical profession.

There's another aspect of medical education that I found disturbing. We spent weeks not only learning about chronaxie and rheobase, but also dissecting a cadaver's hand and foot. How does the knowledge of the bony attachments of those tendons help the average doctor? How does chronaxie or rheobase help in understanding the way the body works, especially if taught so early in the medical course, when students are unfamiliar with basic concepts? And if they are indeed important, the onus falls upon the teacher to explain why this is so and to relate the theory to its practical significance. Certainly, a sense of purpose and proportion is required. For example, a medical student hardly learns enough about ordinary mental disorders even today.

Our medical system continues to function in an ivory tower. Attempts to revise the curriculum often do not achieve their objective because of the sheer resistance to change. Sometimes, our curriculum reflects vested interests by focusing on certain specialty areas of medicine for centuries. What about other aspects of medicine? For example, isn't it unfortunate that an average medical student in India and many other countries does not learn how to assess pain, or manage it?[*] And the teachers are themselves unaware that the students do not know.

True, the World Health Organization (WHO) policy on pain management is tucked away in some corner of the medical textbook. In the first place, it took more than twenty years to make its way into medical textbooks. But is it put into practice? Not by a long shot. Perhaps, 5 per cent of medical colleges in India have introduced pain assessment and management as part of the curriculum of their own accord. And, finally, from 2019, the Indian medical student began to learn about pain management. It is a significant beginning, but it is still a drop in the ocean. The management of other symptoms, for example—another vital aspect of care for someone with serious health-related suffering—is yet to be included in medical curriculum.

---

[*]Alison M. Vargovich, Matthew E. Schumann, Jun Xiang, et al., 'Difficult Conversations: Training Medical Students to Assess, Educate, and Treat the Patient with Chronic Pain', *Academic Psychiatry*, Vol. 43, No. 5, 2019, pp. 494–98.

FIVE

SCREAMS THAT STAYED WITH ME

I would wake up at 4.30 a.m. every morning and negotiate the tricky terrain from my home in Muttacaud to the bus stop to board a bus at 5.45 a.m. It used to take me nearly an hour and a half to reach medical college after boarding another bus at the heart of Trivandrum city. It would be nearly 7 p.m. by the time I returned home in the evening, having endured the jostling crowds in the bus. I used to be so tired that I would doze off even as I pored over my medical books.

And, just as I was dropping off to sleep, the screams would begin. In the silence of the night, it would pierce through every heart in an otherwise silent village neighbourhood. The screams belonged to a distant cousin who lived about a hundred metres away from my house. He had an unusual cancer of the sweat glands and tumours on his scalp. This caused him a lot of pain. He said it was as though someone was drilling through his skull. Even in the mid-1960s, he had received chemotherapy. And, as happens even now, he did not receive any pain relief.

When the family had asked the doctor if they could give him something to relieve the pain, they met with looks of disbelief. 'How can you expect cancer to be pain free?' The idea of easing the agonizing pain of a cancer patient was alien to doctors at that time. It was only in 1967 that a British nurse-turned-physician, Cicely Saunders, opened St Christopher's Hospice, the first modern hospice, in London. She was the one who would introduce effective pain management to the medical community and insist that dying people deserved dignity, compassion, and respect.

I visited my ailing cousin just once, when I was in my first year at medical college. The family knew I was a medical student and wondered if I could help. They asked me if I could do something to ease his pain—but I could do nothing. I shook my head, mumbled something meaningless and walked away. I never visited him again until his death.

I carry that guilt to this day. I could not relieve his pain, but at least I could have held his hand and sat near him for a few minutes. We were never close, but he was my cousin. Why did I never visit him again?

Today, in retrospect, I know why I never visited him again. It was fear. I was afraid of my helplessness and that made me stay away. It hurts me even today to think about him.

A majority of medical students learnt to build a wall of indifference around themselves to shield them from suffering and pain in the first year of clinical studies itself. It was a calculated indifference we developed when we were confronted with human agony. It was rare for a student to stop and help a patient in suffering. Only an odd student would actually buy a meal for a starving patient deserted by his family. The norm was to turn the other way.

It is a sad truth that even today there is so much needless suffering in our hospitals that overwhelm the staff, including doctors. Most of us, as medical students, learn from our teachers and seniors to develop a protective veneer of 'studied insensitivity'. Nobody articulates it in so many words, but the lesson passed on to us is that our job is to diagnose and to cure. We have nothing to do with human suffering. Suffering is inevitable. We better learn to take it philosophically. As for me though, my cousin's screams would come back to haunt me, and change the course of my life.

SIX

THE GOOD AND THE BAD

Looking back on my years as a medical student, I have great reverence for the great teacher–doctors and role models that we had. The most unpleasant of my memories from the time have to do with a few senior doctors who were insensitive towards human suffering and were bereft of empathy, or even compassion.

Most people flocked to government hospitals since they were cheaper, almost free of charge, but they were few and far between in those days. Some avoided our medical college hospital because it was rumoured to 'use' patients to teach medical students.

Private practice for doctors in government hospitals was legal. They were free to offer paid consultations to patients at their residences after hospital hours. The official clinic time for the general public was from 8 a.m. to 1 p.m. in our hospital. Some doctors would arrive late and disappear by noon neglecting the job the government paid them to do. The rest of the day was devoted by many to their private practice.

What infuriated me was the customary consultation fee these doctors quietly took in their clinics before doing a surgery or any other prolonged medical procedure in the government hospital. An arrogant, and bossy, professor took a 'consultation fee' of Rs 25—which was not a small amount at that time—to operate on my mother at the government hospital. The professor knew that I was a medical student at the same hospital and still accepted that fee from my family. I wanted to yell at him: 'I am your student; don't you care what I think of you?' But we students were not courageous enough to complain about these practices and disturb the status quo. It was an act akin to the way we averted our faces to the pain and suffering of patients in our hospital.

Perhaps, nobody saw it as a bribe. Doctors were treated like gods and were entitled to special privileges. I should hasten to add that the majority of doctors were honest and sincere, and did not participate in such corrupt practices.

After passing my exam, I became a house surgeon (intern) for a year, practising medicine under supervision. I had to now plunge deep into a world of suffering that I could avoid as a medical student. Patients approaching the government medical college hospital were poor except those in the pay wards. They were not treated with a lot of compassion. The hospital was terribly understaffed. There were just two nurses for more than sixty patients. In a ward with sixty beds, there would be another sixty patients lying on the floor. The patient had to be critically ill or have influential people to make recommendations on their behalf if they wanted to be upgraded from the floor to a bed. Alternatively, in some wards, the patient's family or friends bribed the staff to gain such an upgrade.

The small number of corrupt doctors stood out conspicuously in the hospital because of the grave injustices they oversaw or perpetrated. There was an oft-discussed story among medical students in my time about a particular surgeon. He would only do a first-step surgery instead of the planned definitive surgery if what the family had paid him did not meet his expectations. This would result in weeks or months of suffering and more expense for the patient.

We learnt to live with these practices. At the same time, we respected the majority of doctors and staff members who staunchly refused to be part of this rot.

◆

Eventually, it was my turn to be offered a bribe. I was the house surgeon in a busy ward and emergency admissions were streaming in. A young man arrived in bad shape after a snake bite. He was delirious and urgently needed an antidote to neutralize the snake venom. Unfortunately, the medicine was not available in the hospital. That was the way the system worked, or rather did not work. Often, in the middle of the night, during an emergency, we would find that we had run out of essential life-saving drugs.

It was way past office hours and the main hospital of the pharmacy was closed. The wife of the man was wailing and his child looked on with terrified eyes, before the hospital security bundled them out leaving only the patient's father to cope with the situation.

I walked across to the government quarters where the doctor in charge of stores lived. The poor man must have been looking forward to a quiet evening with his family when I arrived at his doorstep. I was too timid to be forceful and so merely requested him to give me the antivenin. I must have looked very desperate for he agreed to help me, but not without muttering something under his breath about people being a nuisance. He was merely venting his frustration; he was a good man at heart. We walked back to the hospital. He opened the store and found the antivenin. As he handed it to me, I said, 'Thank you, sir.' I noticed his eyes had lost some harshness.

In a couple of days, the patient sat up and smiled. I felt a huge sense of achievement. Certainly, it did not make me a medical genius as there was little intellectual effort in what I did. But, if I had not taken the trouble to get the stores incharge to do something clearly beyond his duty, the man would have died. The young woman would have become a widow, and the child with the terrified eyes would have had to grow up without a father. I had not performed a miracle, but I had saved a life.

I walked to the ward where the stores incharge worked and told him that the patient was better and thanked him once again. There was the faintest smile on his stern face as he nodded. I felt as if I had won a trophy.

Then came the not-so-pleasant sequel. The patient's father approached me and manoeuvred me to a corner of the ward. He then covertly pressed a ten-rupee currency note into my hand—the first bribe to be offered to me. I recoiled, as if the note had stung me. I remember thrusting it back at him, fuming as I did so. He appeared baffled.

Today, when I look back, I realize that he was doing what he thought was expected of him. There was corruption all around the hospital. Why would he imagine I was different?

To me, the disappointment was considerable. For forty-eight hours, I had been on cloud nine. I had saved a life. I was a doctor, and it meant a great deal to me. When the man put a price on a service, that I believed was what any doctor with a semblance of empathy would have done, I crashed headlong. It was as if he thought the only reason I saved his son was to earn extra money.

◆

The next year, after completing my internship, I began working in a private hospital where I witnessed gross exploitation of patients. I did not want to be a part of it but had to learn to live with it. I saw then what I see even today, the huge imbalance of power—power of the medical knowledge that a doctor holds over a completely powerless person struck down by a disease.

I was later offered two government jobs simultaneously. One was in the General Health Services where I would be the sole doctor in a primary health centre. I would be the boss with several people working under me. The other offer was from the medical education department—I would be a tutor in a medical college. I would also be the junior-most member of the medical staff and be shunted around several departments.

I remember discussing my options with a doctor from my senior batch. He was not a great friend, but someone I happened to meet casually in the college cafeteria. We got talking over a cup of tea. I asked him about his experience as the doctor in a primary health centre. He told me what he had learned from his six months at the centre. 'If you try to be kind, you are doomed. Be ruthless from day one. No one will be thankful even if you are very good. The health centre has such poor facilities that people will be unhappy anyway. Create the impression that you are very corrupt. Build a reputation that you will not give proper treatment to anyone who doesn't bribe you. Then people will start paying you.'

I was flabbergasted. Was this why I had spent six years studying medicine? Disgusted, I finished my tea and stood up to leave.

'Wait,' he said. Here comes the clincher, I thought.

'Let me give you one more piece of advice. The health centre hardly has any medicines. If the patient needs medicines, they will have to buy it from private pharmacies. Patients won't like that and will be angry with you. At the beginning of the month, go personally to the district headquarters and become friends with the stores person. He may get you a few vials of vitamin B-complex injection. Don't give the vitamin injection to anyone. Instead, put in the contents of one ampule into a 500-millilitre bottle of saline. It will look yellow. People like injections. Give them two millilitres of the yellow stuff as an intramuscular injection. And then if you say, "You need a couple more medicines and you have to buy them from outside," they won't mind. They'll be happy that they got the injection free.'

I am sure this practice does not exist today. And perhaps it was unwise of me to have made a judgment based on the counsel of one of the most unsuitable persons around. Nevertheless, that tête-à-tête clinched my decision. The general health service was not for me. I decided to take the academic route.

◆

Today, competition is much stiffer than in my time, and young doctors are faced with many dilemmas. If given the option, many join a service that permits ethical medical practice and earn a decent salary by Indian standards. The salary may not enable them to drive luxury cars, unless one starts accepting unauthorized payments from patients or from unscrupulous elements in the healthcare industry. As they specialize further and become great medical scientists, they will have many more opportunities and temptations to amass wealth.

I once heard of a great clinician who, having retired from the government service, was immediately scooped up by a big corporate hospital. For the hospital, he was a great catch. He was a popular doctor and many patients followed him to his new place of work. He settled in and tried to get used to a completely new work environment.

A couple of months later, one evening, when he had just finished seeing his patients in the outpatient clinic, the suave and personable human resources (HR) assistant manager called on him. She was all praise for his popularity and said how lucky the hospital was to have secured his services. He did not know that he was being fed the routine 'sandwich feedback' (a bitter filling cleverly sandwiched between two sweet slices). 'But doctor, we are concerned that you are not ordering enough MRI scans. We have invested so much into this new equipment. Surely, more patients could benefit from them. Do please cooperate, doctor.' Then came the other sweet slice, 'But doctor, we are so lucky to have you on our staff. You must be an exceptionally good doctor to be so popular. Thank you for being with us.'

The doctor decided that he did not want to have any part in burdening patients with any treatment cost that was unnecessary. He had always resisted any pressure from the healthcare industry and had consistently refused offers of 'sponsored lectures' though it included, in one instance, a trip to Paris for his wife and him. He was not going to start doing this now. If the management came back to him insisting on any unethical practice, he would leave.

But, no more sandwiches came. What he got was a written order moving his outpatient clinic from prime time, 4–7 p.m., to an hour at 2 p.m., when only a few patients would come to the hospital. He took the hint and resigned.

The change from a public-centred healthcare system to a corporate healthcare industry has been the cause of the financial destruction of an almost unbelievably large number of Indians, patients as well as their families. It is a growing phenomenon globally, and particularly so in India. In a 2018 article published in the *British Medical Journal*, Sakthivel Selvaraj and colleagues say that 55 million Indians are pushed below poverty line by catastrophic health expenditure in just one year.[*] What is our healthcare system doing to human health? Health being physical, social, and mental well-being— is the system not destroying the health of those 55 million people and their succeeding generations?

With all the competition young doctors face today, they must be finding it more difficult to practise medicine ethically. When some of them succumb to the pressures and join the bandwagon of unethical practices, the medical profession loses respect and, more importantly, the fallen doctors lose their self-respect. They will then start making excuses such

---

[*]Sakthivel Selvaraj, Habib Hasan Farooqui, and Anup Karan, 'Quantifying the financial burden of households' out-of-pocket payments on medicines in India: a repeated cross-sectional analysis of National Sample Survey data', 1994–2014, *BMJ Open*, Vol. 8, No. 5, 31 May 2018.

as, 'The entire society is corrupt. After all, I am doing this for sheer survival.'

Well, I am glad I took the decision to join the government medical college, which permitted me to live comfortably on my salary, if not in great luxury.

THE MAKING OF AN ANAESTHESIOLOGIST

Work is love made visible.

—Kahlil Gibran[*]

---

[*]From 'On Work', available at <poets.org/ poem/work-4>.

SEVEN

FALLING IN LOVE

I had fallen head over heels in love when I was a house surgeon. I was quite an interesting figure by then, standing tall at 160 centimetres, weighing forty-five kilograms, forever threatening to disappear with a strong wind. Besides my small frame, Mother Nature had also endowed me with buck teeth, which gave me an enormous inferiority complex. Feeling quite apologetic, my inadequate upper lip would involuntarily try to cover them up every few seconds, and, fail miserably. Many years later, my friend and dental surgeon Dr Abraham Thomas worked on my upper incisors and using some of those deadly weapons that only dental surgeons are licensed to carry, sawed off an inch or so of each of them allowing me to smile at the world without inhibition.

I had never considered myself an Adonis. My relationship with the opposite sex had been practically non-existent except for my batchmates in the hospital, who were mostly gentle and compassionate girls who seemed to tolerate me as an unfortunate accident of nature. Chandrika was the first one to take me seriously. She had the most lilting giggles and, God, I loved them.

Wait a minute. This story is not about my love life. My romance creeps into this story only because it had a decisive role on my medical career. Chandrika had taken up a government job in the faraway city of Calicut. It would take me twelve hours by bus to reach Calicut from Trivandrum, my hometown. Luckily, I was called for an interview for a 'provisional' job in the Calicut Medical College.

I got to Calicut, presented myself for the interview, and the principal said, 'Go to obstetrics and gynaecology. OK?'

I was hoping I could get into internal medicine and timidly mentioned my preference.

'No,' he said, 'They badly need people in obstetrics. If you want the job, you must take it.'

I took it, of course. I would have taken any job whatsoever, if only I could be in the same institution as Chandrika.

I stayed in obstetrics and gynaecology for about six months. It was not my cup of tea, I was sure, but I was able to get along. Dr E. K. Varghese and Dr Bhadran were kind and friendly professors and taught me what I needed to know. Well, I stuck to it. There were compensations.

As members of the teaching staff, I could not walk around the campus with Chandrika, the way an occasional student couple might. We would sneak away on Sunday mornings to watch a movie together, or to Queen's restaurant near the beach to have a meal together, before catching a bus back to our respective hostels.

The six-day weeks were busy, with a monthly weekend duty thrown in for good measure.

I remember being halfway through doing a post-partum sterilization on a woman when a voice from behind me said, 'You have been ousted.' This was technical language. It meant that a permanent appointee had come to occupy my chair and I had to leave the department. The system was flexible enough to permit me to stay until I sewed the wound up. With a sigh of relief, I left the department.

Now the drill was another interview with the principal. This time I knew better. I would not ask for anything specific. But, I was sure of one thing—I did not want to be an anaesthesiologist. This came out of my observations as a house surgeon. Surgeons did such wonderful things, cutting and sewing, orchestrating the entire operation and holding forth. They were the miracle workers. Meanwhile, you would have a person seated at the head of the table endlessly squeezing a bag—the bag that would breathe for the patient who has been paralysed by anaesthesia. I couldn't think of a more boring job.

So when the principal asked, 'What department do you want?' I had my answer ready: 'Anything sir, except anaesthesia.'

'You don't like anaesthesia?' I didn't like the look on his face, but I nodded. He delivered the verdict: 'You go to anaesthesia.' And, that was that. There was no court of appeal.

I formally became a staff member in the department of anaesthesiology. Then and today, young doctors don't often have the opportunity to choose the medical stream they want. When they are left with no reasonable choice, many settle down to whatever field they have chanced upon. I was lucky; I ended up doing something that I learnt to like. But, I worry, as a patient, would I end up being treated by a doctor who dislikes his work?

I was ready to be bored to death. Yet, I could not control my nervous excitement when I first stepped into the operating theatre (OT). I was lucky; I had a guide, Dr Kumar, who was another provisional appointee. He was a few months senior to me in the department and looked knowledgeable and in complete command. Just as a child would hang on to the folds of his mother's clothes, I clung to my senior.

There were hurdles in my path. A tussle was on between two professors about who was in charge of the department. The government red tape required me to prepare three copies of the charge transfer certificate (CTC) and get them signed by the department head. But how was I to know who was the head? The issue had not been resolved by the people in power.

I went to one of the two professors and said, 'I have come to join the department.'

'Bring me the CTC forms. I will sign them.' The emphasis on the 'I' warned me of danger.

Kumar saved me. 'That's okay. Now go to the other professor and tell him the same.' So I did that.

He too said, 'Bring me the CTC forms to sign.'

Kumar the wise, advised me, 'Go to the admin office and get six blank forms. Get three signed by one and three by the other. Then take them all to the office and dump them there. Let them choose what they want.'

O, Kumar, the omniscient, you were my saviour! As it turned out, this was excellent advice. I escaped without getting embroiled in the rows that some of my predecessors had got into.

The main medical college hospital had an urgent need for an anaesthesiologist and that's where I went. The kind professor, who was our supervisor, told Kumar, 'Teach him what to do.' Then he turned to me and added, 'You must be a fast learner. Next week, you will be on your own in an OT.' It all looked simple enough. I thought there would not be too much to learn. Kumar took me with him to the OT in the general surgery unit.

Those were the days when Indian hospitals were just changing over from the old-fashioned anaesthetic agents like ether to the more sophisticated, 'balanced' anaesthesia with muscle relaxants and nitrous oxide. There was also one machine in the hospital that could administer the fearfully expensive halothane and, of course, we juniors could not touch it. Kumar taught me not to go into the OT too early in the morning—'They will take you for granted'—and never too late—'You will get pounced on'.

The routine of surgical anaesthesia started with intravenous thiopentone most of the time. As the medicine flowed in, the patient would become unconscious in seconds. We would then inject a short-acting muscle relaxant called suxamethonium, which would paralyse the patient and stop the breathing for about five minutes. The anaesthesiologists then blew oxygen into the lungs with a mask and bag, and then needed all the skill we possessed to open the mouth, use a laryngoscope to view the voice box, and push a red rubber endotracheal tube through it.

If you kept yourself in the good books of the anaesthesia technician, you would get a tube with a working cuff, so that gas wouldn't leak around the tube and the patient would not be at risk of aspirating the deadly gastric contents. Then you would partially paralyse the person with a little gallamine, a longer acting muscle relaxant. This was important; because without it, the patient could cough. If the surgery did not involve the abdomen, and if a lot of relaxation was not required, the patients could breathe on their own with a combination of oxygen and nitrous oxide with ether. The initiation with ether was always tough. It was an irritant and the patient would often cough horribly; you had to give just enough gallamine to keep the person from coughing. The surgeon would plead for more relaxation.

Kumar advised me to push a bit of normal saline into the vein and to tell the surgeon that I had administered the relaxation. 'Whatever you do or don't do, they will stitch them up somehow and immediately walk away. You will be the one left to get the patient to start breathing again,' was my sagacious guide's advice.

Unfortunately, that was the worst possible advice and training that I could have received as a novice anaesthesiologist. I learned to do things the Kumar way.

In about six months, quite coincidentally, I was offered a 'permanent' position in a department of anaesthesia in my alma mater in Trivandrum. A permanent appointment was an act of God which could not be ignored. I had to leave Chandrika and my provisional job, say goodbye to Calicut for the time being, and return to Trivandrum to be an anaesthesiologist.

In Trivandrum, I was assigned to the obstetrics and gynaecology operation theatre. The jovial and knowledgeable Dr Anantha Padmanabhan, fondly called AP, was in charge. AP could laugh at anything and correct us without offending anyone. I felt quite well-informed in anaesthesia and was eager to demonstrate my skills to my new boss. He came with me to the OT to watch me inducing anaesthesia in a patient. At the end of the procedure, he took me back to his office and told me with a kind smile, 'Rajagopal, forget everything that you have learnt so far about anaesthesia. We are going to make a new beginning.' Somehow, I trusted him implicitly. I was very happy to leave the rather barbaric practices that I had become used to and to start practising safer and more humane anaesthetic techniques.

I started loving anaesthesiology. It was by no means glamorous. The benevolent but tough head of department, Dr Surendran was always encouraging.

What they say about anaesthesia is often true—it is ninety per cent boredom and ten per cent sheer panic. When you anaesthetize someone, you have to depress his bodily functions. We still do not have the miracle drug which can simply make the person unconscious and leave all other bodily functions undisturbed. The trick is to make the brain depressed enough, but at the same time, keep all the organs functioning as normally as possible. It was in Trivandrum that it dawned on me that anaesthesiologists often require greater skill than many other clinicians. The act of keeping a patient's bodily functions stable during surgery and bringing them around to a normal state at the end of the procedure is a daunting challenge.

I could see that patients behaved differently at the end of the surgery. Some would wake up screaming and fighting, while others would be calm and comfortable. To me, much of this difference seemed to be related to the skill of the anaesthesiologist.

The science of anaesthesiology evolved in an effort to keep patients free of pain. It is obvious that the same principles with suitable modifications would help to treat pain in many other situations. Anaesthesiologists need to remember that they are doctors whose duty is to relieve suffering. It would be a shame if they consider it their duty to merely make patients unconscious and immobile during surgery and not take the trouble to ensure their well-being after the operation. They also have to make sure the patients are not in pain, for the agony after a surgery can often be unbearable.

It was exciting to see the difference an anaesthesiologist could make through minute-by-minute interventions. Primarily, our job was to keep the patients as unaffected as possible by the surgical procedures they were undergoing. And, the greatest achievement was when a patient smiled at you, awake and pain-free at the end of an operation, and asked, 'Is it over?'

The practice of anaesthesiology didn't bring us many bouquets, but I understood it played a key role in the patient's safety and well-being.

EIGHT

DOCTORS ONLY SEE THE DISEASE

Chandrika and I belonged to different castes. An inter-caste relationship was not taken lightly in those days; but we were revolutionaries and finally got married. Our reluctant families joined the modest ceremony, which had all the cheer of an average funeral. There was no wedding feast. The extended family took some time to get used to the caste difference, but some sort of peace was eventually restored.

A year later, I got selected for a postgraduate degree course at the All India Institute of Medical Sciences in New Delhi. When I returned to Trivandrum as a specialist in anaesthesiology, I kept thinking of my cousin in my village, whose screams would keep us awake at night. I have never been able to shake off that guilty feeling whenever I think of him. I wanted to see if I could apply some of my knowledge that I had gained after the course to relieve pain outside the operation theatre as well. A friend of mine who knew about my interest in pain management sent Shekhar to me.

This incident occurred thirty-five years ago, but I can still vividly recall Shekhar's eyes. He had the look of a hunted animal, but harboured hope in his eyes. I thought I could help Shekhar with the knowledge I had picked up on the theory of nerve blockades. He had a severe obstruction to some blood vessels in his body. I do not remember the diagnosis, but the physicians and surgeons had signed off on the verdict—it was not treatable. A doctor friend had however recommended him to see an anaesthesiologist who might be able to help. His big toe had turned blue and was beginning to get gangrenous. He was young and did not want his toe to be amputated.

When a blood vessel or blood vessels get blocked by a disease or clots, often the body tries to compensate by opening up smaller blood vessels. We call them collateral blood vessels. Somehow, enough blood was still passing through the collaterals to keep the blood flowing to the rest of the limb, but the big toe had given up. Because of such obstructions in the blood vessels, the pain experienced is among the worst kind, and is not at all easy to treat.

At that time, treatment for pain relief was non-existent. This was years before the WHO's three-step ladder for pain medicines was born. I decided if I injected a local anaesthetic agent into the right group of nerves, I could determine whether practically destroying the nerve with a chemical would relieve the pain. It should, I thought. I had seen the procedure described in my anaesthesiology textbook.

Shekhar was already hospitalized. I was most keen to insert an epidural catheter and see if I could relieve his pain. I could think about the next steps later. For now, I was not sure if he could retain his sanity for another day.

But, I received a shock when permission was denied to me by my superior. 'We have enough work in the operating theatres. We cannot afford to have you start working in the wards,' he said.

I did not have the courage to fight. I gave in (and feel ashamed that I did). I apologized to Shekhar that I could not help him in any way. The worst thing was that there was no other doctor to whom I could refer him.

I sat there and watched as the last sign of hope drained from Shekhar's face. He sat with a downcast face for another moment, and with drooping shoulders limped out of the room. I never saw him again and I never enquired what had happened to him. I did not want to. I was myself in pain.

After all this time, not much has changed. Except for a tiny minority (less than 4 per cent),[*] most people with pain in India continue to suffer needlessly, though for many decades now, medical science has the solutions. Compassionate doctors who want to help in this kind of situation continue to be forced to turn away from suffering in the face of a lopsided medical education and practice, which focus only on the disease to the exclusion of everything else, including suffering. I was beginning to see that as doctors we are taught to see only the disease, not the human being who has it.

---

[*] F. M. Knaul, P. E. Farmer, E. L. Krakeur, et al., 'Alleviating the access abyss in palliative care and pain relief—an imperative of universal health coverage: the *Lancet* Commission report', *The Lancet*, Vol. 391, Issue 10128, 12 October 2017.

NINE

MORRIS, THE HARBINGER OF LIGHT

In the early 1980s, after Chandrika and I had completed building our own nest, we had no savings left. My son Abhi was just a year old and Chandrika was pregnant with Anu. It was not a good time to leave home. Yet, sheer greed made me extract a leave of absence from a not-too-eager Kerala Government to work with the ministry of defence in the Sultanate of Oman for three years. My friend Radhakrishnan (BRK to all his friends) had found me the job; he was no admirer of my honest poverty.

And that was what brought me to one of my teachers in pain management, Morris. It was my second year in Oman. I was the lone anaesthesiologist in a small military hospital in Salalah. This was much before I had discovered palliative care, when I was steeped in my mainstream anaesthesiology and critical care work.

Morris, a civilian cook from Bangladesh, had been severely injured when a gas cylinder exploded at his workplace. The only areas on his body to escape serious burns were his face, head, and the area covered by his khaki shorts—70 per cent of his body had been burnt. He was in his late twenties; so age was in his favour.

The Salalah hospital meanwhile was not adequately equipped to treat people with such extensive burns. In the absence of a specialized burn care division at the hospital, as an anaesthesiologist with an interest in intensive care, it fell on me to be his primary care physician.

I did not have much expert help, but I did have access to many willing hands. Several nurses came forward to help beyond their call of duty. Together, we looked after Morris.

Burns on 70 per cent of a body bring with them a lot of pain. I had no significant training in pain management, especially in those days before the birth of the now famous WHO analgesic ladder.[*] In addition to the pain and suffering, the days following a severe burn are extremely challenging. The kidneys are at grave risk because of the by-products of tissue destruction. Nutrition and hydration of the patient also have to be meticulously monitored.

Fortunately, the top half of Morris's neck was spared. I could manipulate a central venous catheter into a large vein in his neck and move its tip close to his heart to be able to measure his central venous pressure. This was very helpful in balancing his hydration. But a catheter like that also posed the threat of possible infection, especially when an area so close to its site of insertion was burned and also likely to get infected. I discarded this intervention as soon as his kidneys appeared to be no longer at risk.

I tried to treat his pain with rather high doses of morphine. Luckily, injectable morphine was available to me. But I was afraid. The man was young and would probably require pain relief for weeks and weeks. Would I turn him

---

[*]WHO, 'Cancer Pain Relief', 1986, available at <https://apps.who.int/iris/bitstream/handle/10665/43944/9241561009_eng.pdf;jsessionid=D547508ADFAA41F72A0CDB13F4398D72?seque nce=1>.

into an addict? At that time, I did not know that if you balance the opioid dose to the degree of pain, especially if given orally, the chances of addiction are low. Based on the rather inane notion (now I know better) that switching opioids every few days would decrease the risk of addiction; I decided I would also give him pethidine (meperidine, a pain reliever) as well. Also, for the same reason, I decided to withdraw his pain relief medicine intermittently to prevent him from getting addicted. I only gave it to him when he was writhing in severe pain; I really made him earn his morphine or pethidine.

During this period, Morris and I became friends. His family was in Bangladesh and he was lonely in Oman. He regaled me with stories of his family; about his uncommon name in Bangladesh, and about his daughter. She was the star in his life and featured heavily in his stories. He nurtured this dream to return to a normal life and to his family.

Eventually, after a couple of months, he was transferred to a hospital in another city for plastic surgery. I did not see Morris for another two months but received reports about his recovery. Meanwhile, I had received a lot of compliments. It was not easy to treat someone with such severe burns under the circumstances and for the patient to survive. Both outcomes made me happy: the fact that he was better and would see his wife and child again, and the fact that I was able to achieve something substantial. I couldn't wait to see him again.

When I did meet him finally, I expected him to be effusive in his gratitude towards me. I had pictured him choked up with emotion as he thanked me for saving his life. Instead, I was flabbergasted by his reaction.

Morris looked at me for a long moment and then said, 'You almost destroyed me.'

I was shocked and deeply hurt. What was happening here? Hadn't I saved his life? The nurses and I had spent sleepless nights to ensure he survived despite the lack of medical facilities to treat him for his kind of burns. It was nothing short of a miracle to me.

I asked him with trepidation, 'What do you mean?'

'I was in agony for months in this wretched hospital as well. Couldn't you at least reduce my pain?' he asked bitterly. 'You just gave me few hours of pain relief every now and then. Why weren't you more liberal with it? Do you have any idea how much I suffered?'

My inflated but fragile ego shattered like glass. I thought he was being ungrateful, but said nothing. Morris walked away. I never saw him again.

It took me a long time to understand what had happened with Morris. He was right. Every word he had said was true. He had deserved pain relief round the clock. I had the means to provide it to him but, in my ignorance, I had rationed it.

Today, when I see my fellow professionals who either refuse to offer pain relief or ration it needlessly, I think of Morris. I was ignorant then about pain and its management. They are ignorant now.

Doctors who have had a chance to see the light have the responsibility to advocate for pain relief measures and encourage the use of opioids in a safe and appropriate manner. The medical system has to change and accept the principle of balance—the need to make opioids available to those who need them for pain relief while taking steps to prevent inappropriate or non-medical use.

We need to teach healthcare professionals and students that their primary duty of care (as officially defined in India) is to 'mitigate suffering. It is to cure sometimes, relieve often. and comfort always.... There exists no exception to this rule.'*

Morris was one of my teachers. He made me see the light.

---

*ICMR, 2018, available at <https://main.icmr.nic.in/sites/default/files/Books/Definition_of_terms_used_in_limitation_of_treatment_and_providing_palliative_care_at_end_of_life.pdf>.

TEN

AWAKENING TO PAIN

Three years later, in 1986, when I felt I had wriggled my way well above the poverty line, I returned to India. I did not want to miss out on the growing up years of my two sons. And I felt India was where my work would be most meaningful.

As anaesthesiology was not a too sought-after specialty at that time, competition was minimal and I moved up the ladder rapidly to become a professor, no less. In the government service, it was not really a question of climbing the ladder. You just stayed in the queue without creating waves, and the momentum or the lack of it simply pushed you up. It was merely a question of seniority.

The powers that be sent my wife and me back to the medical college in the northern Kerala city of Calicut, where we moved into the government quarters on the campus with our two young sons. I was the head of anaesthesiology. The work was hard since the department was always grossly understaffed, but I had several excellent team members.

In an effort to improve patient care and make a difference, we started a preanaesthesia clinic. Space was always at a premium in the sprawling, overcrowded 2000-bed hospital. We ran the clinic in the corridor outside the operating theatre. Patients would come in before an operation for a preanaesthetic evaluation by the anaesthesiologist at the clinic after their doctors had completed their ward rounds. The anaesthesiologist would do a physical examination, scan through the investigations, prescribe a preanaesthetic medication for the night and one for the morning of the operation, and the patient would head back to the ward. We should have interacted with anxious patients in a more comfortable and calming environment but this was the only space available at the time.

That was where I found Babu one day, crouched under an examination table. The man's curled-up posture was so striking that I went up to him immediately and knelt down to talk to him. He shrank back in fright almost into the wall—I learnt later that the slightest touch or even a gentle breeze blowing over his arm was unbelievable torture to him.

As it turned out, his suffering was totally avoidable. He had met with a traffic accident in which his hand had been injured and he had been taken to a hospital. The staff was about to report the accident to the police, when, sensing trouble, Babu vanished from the scene and went to a quack for treatment.

The human hand is a dangerous place to have an infection in. It can travel deep into the spaces between different planes of tissue and can spread elsewhere, and that is exactly what had happened. The quack continued treating Babu until he had no money left, by which time his forearm was badly infected. He finally arrived at the medical college hospital where, after evaluations and several weeks of treatment, the surgeons had decided to amputate his arm.

Babu welcomed it—anything was welcome if it took away

his pain. In the meantime, he waited, crouched under a table, desperately hoping the world would not touch him even with the best of intentions.

I could not simply prescribe a preanaesthetic medication and send him away. Here was a human being in agony, who needed emergency treatment. Preanaesthetic and preoperative preparation would be meaningless if we did not take care of his pain. He could barely speak and it fell upon his wife to narrate the story of his unimaginable suffering.

With great reluctance, he allowed me to put an intravenous cannula into his healthy arm. I suppose this was the only time when I cannulated someone's vein crouched under an examination table. Very clearly, Babu had become hypersensitive to pain. Even the jab of the needle necessary to inject local anaesthetic in order to insert the intravenous cannula drew an agonized cry. That is the way continuous unrelieved pain behaves—it winds up the nervous system, making it overly sensitive to any stimulus.

Intravenous pethidine was the only effective injectable opioid we had at that time. It sometimes causes nausea and vomiting, so I decided to give him an anti-emetic first as he wouldn't be able to bear the movement any retching could cause. I followed it up with 10 milligrams of pethidine intravenously, every five minutes.

I do not remember exactly how much I gave him, but with less than 100 milligrams inside him, the man was transformed. With bewildered eyes, and with the greatest expression of joy that I can remember on a human face, he rejoiced, 'You have cured me!'

I hastened to explain that I hadn't cured him. Only the pain had been relieved. But he wasn't listening. 'You work miracles! This is magic! Are you God?' he asked. 'I don't want to go back to my ward. You keep me here. You treat me.'

It took a lot of persuasion to get him to return to his ward, armed with a prescription for painkillers.

He did not turn up for surgery the next morning, but reappeared in the preanaesthesia clinic later in the morning looking for me. There had been an almost unbelievable reduction in the size of his arm. The day before the entire arm was swollen, but a nearly normal-sized arm presented itself now. The surgeon decided to postpone the amputation.

The improvement is not theoretically difficult to explain. Medical science had revealed that unrelieved pain not only progressively worsens the pain, but also contracts blood vessels in that area. So here was a man, with already poor blood flow to the limb experiencing a progressive reduction in blood flow because of this reflex activity. With the pain gone, some collateral blood vessels had apparently opened up, enabling movement and restoring some circulation in the arm.

The improvement, however, was not good enough to save his arm. The infection ran deep and the following week, the surgeon decided to proceed with the amputation.

'So, your miracle was wasted,' the surgeon told me.

I did not argue with him but I knew that my efforts had not been wasted. For one, every minute of pain relief was precious to Babu. Secondly, if he had continued in pain till the time of surgery, he would have been more likely to develop phantom limb pain. This sort of pain is a trick that the brain plays on itself, following the loss of a body part such as a finger, a toe, or a limb. The brain doesn't seem to be able to accept or realize that the body part is lost, and continues adapting its nervous system. The cruel consequence is that a person can continue to feel pain in the non-existent limb. In Babu's case however, I hoped that the phantom limb sensations would be bearable. The post-operative phantom limb pain a person experiences appears to be proportionate to the pain in that limb before surgery.

Babu came back to see me before he was discharged from the hospital. He cried as he held my hand with his remaining one and gave me a blessing. He wished me a long and healthy life, so I would be able to relieve the pain of many more patients like him. I cherish that blessing.

The experience also showed me what a pain crisis actually was, before I had heard the expressions 'pain crisis' and 'pain emergency'. The kind of pain that Babu had undergone needed treatment on an emergency basis. From that time, I started treating excruciating pain with repeated aliquots (for the layperson, it is a portion of a larger whole) of injectable opioids. Usually, I used morphine, because it was inexpensive. It came in 15-milligram ampoules. I would dilute an ampoule into 10 millilitres and give a millilitre every ten minutes. Later, when it became available and time was a constraint, I opted for the more expensive fentanyl (a quick acting morphine-like opioid), giving 10 micrograms every three minutes initially, followed by more injections several times a day. In majority of the cases, this took care of the pain crisis.

Much later, I switched to oral morphine when it became available to us, after tackling the pain emergency.

Babu also taught me that I could use my familiarity with painkillers to relieve human suffering caused by non-surgical pain. It would be a shame to waste the chance to ease even a little suffering.

ELEVEN

THE GENEROUS LISTENER

I was beginning to find some time and mind space to pursue a few things I was keen on.

I could not dislodge the memory of Shekhar from my mind. I can't say I was happy with this long-term tenant in my head, but I could not evict him.

I began working on nerve blocks in earnest. Rather naively, I assumed that the doctors in most clinical departments would know about all the medicines available to treat pain. And, if they could not relieve pain, what medicines were left for me to try? But as an anaesthesiologist, I decided I could try nerve blocks. Few people in the country had tried them to treat pain.

Several years ago, I had heard of Dr M. T. Bhatia, a 'pain pioneer' in Ahmedabad. I had written to him asking whether I could get some pain management training under him. Unfortunately, he was abroad, and the cold, abrupt response from one of his colleagues had discouraged me. Life had yet not taught me the key to success—persistence.

I convinced myself that I could work with nerve blocks without formal training. There were books I could learn from, I told myself. I approached the heads of the two oncology units in the hospital and requested them to refer patients in pain to me, if they thought they would benefit from nerve blocks. Every time I talked to them, a few sporadic patients were referred to me. People with pain in the face were the most common. Cancers of the head and neck were more rampant in India than in many other parts of the world;[*] this was possibly related to tobacco.

Patients with pain in the upper abdomen—say, with cancer of the stomach, pancreas, or organs around them—were amenable to one kind of a nerve block known as coeliac plexus block.

The procedure itself was cruel and painful. In those days, there was no real-time imaging. It had to be done blind, which reduced the chances of success. Yet, I had some remarkable wins as well.

One day Warrier, an elderly man with cancer came to see me. His cancer was considered not to be active at that time since he had responded to treatment. And, I was told, it was a kind of cancer unlikely to spread to his chest. But he had an agonizing pain on one side of his chest. There were no CT scans or sophisticated imaging in those days, and an X-ray was the best we could do. His X-ray was normal. I somehow managed to get several specialists to see him. One of them stood there, discussing the man's problem with him and mechanically kept pressing the painful area with his thumb repeatedly every few seconds till I stopped him. Some doctors were just not sensitive to pain.

But no doctor could demystify the reason for the pain or suggest a solution.

---

[*]Snehal Bhupesh Shah, Shilpi Sharma, and Anil Kieth D'Cruz, 'Head and neck oncology: The Indian scenario', *South Asian J Cancer*, Vol. 5, No. 3, July–September 2016, pp. 104–105.

There was no safe nerve block that could give Warrier any relief for more than a few hours. He asked my opinion on some of his medications; no one else would bother to answer his questions. That was the first time I seriously looked at pain medicines instead of just leaving it to a primary care physician. He said he felt noticeably better after I had tweaked the frequency at which the medicines were given.

One day, Warrier asked me if I could see him once a week. This was not very easy for me, honestly. I had a lot on my plate—I was working in the operation theatre, handling anaesthetic management of major operations, some of which required my personal attention; managing a department with dozens of staff members; and trying to keep my sanity while overseeing the administration of the operation theatres. Electricity, oxygen, anaesthetic gas, and water supply would take turns to frequently fail in the operation theatres. And, it would take colossal time and effort to get them going once again, often with little support from the administration, who had their own challenges to deal with.

Warrier's beseeching face won over my reluctance to help. We talked, and arranged to meet fairly regularly.

'I know you are busy,' he said. 'So I try not to come often, but I really cannot manage without any support now. Even if the medicines do not help, your words give me some solace.'

My words? What words? I hardly spoke. And then it dawned on me—it wasn't my words, it was my ears that he needed. He wanted to unburden his mind and I was willing to listen whenever I could.

He would return every week, sometimes waiting for hours to see me. We had agreed to schedule an X-ray every three months to see if we could discover the reason for his pain. My clinical ability to do this was very limited, but I did it because apparently no one else was willing to do it for him. His own doctor had deserted him a while ago, saying, 'There is nothing wrong with you. It's all in your mind.'

From Warrier, I learnt the value of listening.

The ending of this story is not a happy one. The man, who had been callously diagnosed as having 'nothing wrong with him' medically, dropped dead one day after a severe spell of pain and breathlessness. What he left in his wake, however, was an invaluable lesson for me—that I could be more than just a doctor who does all the talking, and that a doctor must always be ready to listen to the patient.

TWELVE

ARE THERE ANY PATIENTS FOR NERVE BLOCKS?

Whenever I met the two senior oncologists at the medical college in Calicut, I would always badger them with this question (much to their amusement, let me add), 'Do you have any patients suitable for nerve blocks?'

I was quite like the fabled Arjun, from the Hindu epic, the Mahabharata, in those days. Not in looks, I fear—almost on the other end of that spectrum. Nor in courage either, which was one of the things that Arjun was famous for. But in focus.

Drona the guru, had been instructing the princes in archery. He decided to conduct a test.

'I want you to take aim at that bird,' he said and led his pupils one by one to the bow and arrow.

The eldest came by and took position.

'What do you see?' Drona asked.

'I see the tree, its branches and leaves, and the bird seated on one of the topmost branches,' was the reply.

Successive pupils stepping into position gave similar answers. Finally, it was Arjun's turn.

'What do you see, Arjun?' Drona asked.

'I see the eye of the bird.' It was the answer Drona

had been waiting for, and with that response, Arjun passed his Guru's test.

If in nothing else, I was like Arjun in my objective—people in pain would be sent to me now and then, and all I would see were their nerves. I started doing more and more nerve blocks.

I had, with great difficulty, acquired almost pure alcohol which could be injected to destroy the nerve function for an average of six months. The procedure called for long needles. Disposable ones were unavailable in those days. I had also found a set of needles—rather cruel, steel needles autoclaved and reused several times, often dulled by their frequent usage. A person was in front of me, in flesh and blood, in all his defenceless frailty, but I would only see his nerves.

All my training was from books and I used my academic knowledge to unrelentingly poke needles into people's bodies.

But the person in whom these nerves were ensconced would inconveniently refuse to remain in the background and would insist on manifesting to me. My tunnel vision had no choice but to expand.

Though the procedures were often very painful, they turned out to be extremely useful when successful. Cancers of the head and neck were even more common in our country then than they are now and many people lived (and continue to live) with excruciating pain. I had the rare satisfaction of giving significant pain relief to many. While I couldn't exactly tell how or where the pain was neurologically housed, I was always willing to listen to their tales of woe. They felt comforted by my kind act of listening and were as a result more inclined to endure the excruciatingly painful procedures I made them undergo.

There were a few colleagues who were always keen to help. Dr Molly John, who had been temporarily heading the department for the year before I took over, was a true professional. She was also a great friend and turned out to be a solid pillar of support.

In the absence of a designated room to carry out my nerve block procedures, I did most of them in the post-operative room. The adjoining beds would invariably be occupied by patients, who were crying or snoring, and yet, I would stake out a corner bed and do what I needed to.

One day, a forty-two-year-old college professor was referred to me by his cousin, a doctor friend of mine. The man had spent the last two years living with a cancer of the tongue. The radiation had offered him temporary reprieve but now the disease had recurred. Chemotherapy did not seem effective. Could I do something?

Needless to say, the pain was unbearable. The cancer had only minimally deformed his face but he could scarcely speak on account of the pain. It was impossible to completely avoid movements of the tongue, and the slightest movement was agony for him. We did not have oral morphine at that time.

I gave him some codeine. Codeine is, for all practical purposes, weak morphine. It would get converted to morphine in the body and have its effect. It has what we call a ceiling effect however, meaning the dose cannot be increased beyond a certain amount. Codeine was by no means enough for the professor. We agreed to do a mandibular nerve block the next day.

My needle had to weave in and out several times in order to get to the nerve. Regrettably, we needed him to continually report his sensation of pins and needles, and for that essential communication to be able to happen, this procedure could not be done under anaesthesia. I did give him some painkiller, which was hardly adequate.

To his credit, the professor withstood the procedure fairly well. I put in some local anaesthetic while the needle stayed in place. In about five minutes, he had pain relief which confirmed to me that the needle was properly positioned and I proceeded to inject alcohol into the spot.

Despite the agony that he went through, the man was visibly pleased. Hope blossomed bright on his face. He could now live without pain. I warned him that the pain may return in about an hour but would gradually disappear over the next twenty-four hours. I made an appointment to meet him again the following day.

His pain was almost completely gone the next day. For the first time, I saw a smile on his face that actually reached his eyes. I was glad, blissfully unaware that the smile was not going to last long.

When the consultation was over, the professor asked me when he should come back to see me again. 'You don't have to come back,' I told him. 'Of course, if the pain returns, come back then and we shall see what we can do about it.'

His face must have registered some of what he felt then. But I missed it. I was mentally patting myself on the shoulder.

The professor died by suicide that night.

What my colleague, his cousin, told me later was that no one had discussed the prognosis with him. The professor had no idea that there were no curative options left for him. The oncologist had just referred him to me saying that henceforth I would handle his treatment. When I told him that he need not come back, it seemed to confirm what he had suspected for a while. His condition was incurable. For all intents and purposes, my words must have conveyed to him that his pain had been conquered but temporarily. He most likely did not want to go through that pain (or my horrendous needles) ever again. So, he took the only exit he felt he could, leaving behind his young wife and two children.

I felt dejected because I felt responsible. I felt that if only I had listened to the man, or to what he had left unsaid, if only I had recognized his fears maybe that woman would not have been widowed in such a traumatic manner. And maybe, his children could have had their father for a few more months or even a year.

The man gave up his life to teach me a vital lesson. He taught me that doctors should be more than body mechanics—that they also have the tremendous and awesome responsibility of recognizing, acknowledging, and honouring the human beings that entrust their lives to them.

DISCOVERING PALLIATIVE CARE

*To make a great dream come true,
the first requirement is a great capacity to dream;
the second is persistence.*

—Cesar Chavez[*]

---

[*]Quoted in United States of America, 'Proceedings and Debates of the 117th Congress, First Session', *Congressional Record*, Vol. 167, No. 51, 18 March 2021.

THIRTEEN

LETTING HIM GO GENTLY INTO THE NIGHT

Sometimes, we walk a short distance before we realize that we have crossed a pivotal bridge in our lives. I had entered unchartered territory, a terra incognita, sometime in the late 1980s, but I did not yet know it by its true name: palliative care. I had not heard of this term back then, but unknowingly I had plunged headlong into it.

Little did I know that this incredible work had already made its way to India. Dr Luzito DeSouza, an onco-surgeon, had by now built the first hospice in the country: Shanti Avedna Sadan in Mumbai. I just hadn't heard about it. I was essentially treating physical pain, but while I did that, my patients also shared their stories and their suffering with me, equipping me with a new kind of insight that allowed me to consider and discover their internal worlds. Their stories were altering and shaping my own inner mindscape, propelling me to do what I could to ease their suffering.

There were lessons to be learnt every day; new territory to navigate. One morning as I walked into the operation theatre corridor several minutes before the official work hours commenced, I found a patient lying on a trolley sobbing hysterically. It was hard to tell how long she had been left like that. It suited the system for the ward staff on night duty, in their eagerness to go home, to transport patients needing surgery to the operation theatre much before their turn. However, sometimes the unfortunate patient would have to lie alone on their trolleys along corridors outside the operation theatre for more than an hour. Their families were certainly not allowed anywhere near them. It was a lonely kind of hell.

I approached the crying woman. As soon as I touched her arm, she clung to me and implored, 'Please, let me see my son once more. They brought me here before he arrived. I think I'm going to die during the operation and I will never get to see him again. Please help me see him just once.' It was a simple thing to roll the trolley out into the waiting area where the relatives were all huddled. I shall never forget the look on her face as she hugged her son.

In those days, pain was a constant spectre haunting corridors and hallways, wards and rooms. Hospitals, where pain was generally left untreated, were its playground. I imagine that the preoperative period must have been particularly hard for those in pain, especially when left to contend with their misery on their own. Occasionally, I did attempt to help, and gave them small doses of injectable morphine, and if the dose was not enough, I would give them some more a little later, as I had done for Babu.

This was not some ingenious method, but I suppose in some ways it was also new in our practice at that time. There was nothing unscientific about what I was doing. The small bolus of morphine that I gave could relieve pain and couldn't possibly cause any significant harm.

I had looked up a couple of books and had found that even when given intravenously, morphine takes time to cross into the brain cells, which is where it really works its special kind of magic. It could take fifteen minutes to half an hour for the drug to meander its way up the arteries and cross the blood–brain barrier (a protective network of blood vessels and cells that filters blood flowing to the brain). So I would wait for about ten minutes or so before I gave a second dose, hypothesizing that even if I give two tiny doses, marginally exceeding what was strictly necessary, no harm would be done.

The practice of intravenous titration of morphine (or another opioid) against pain has become rather routine today in many palliative care centres in India. A morphine trial, as we call it, is a beauty to behold. Patients come in bent out of shape in pain. They are hooked up to the IV line and given small doses of morphine even as they report their pain on a scale they can relate to. The titration is complete when the patients report that the pain is under control to their satisfaction, and that becomes their magic number on the pain scale. This process does not take very long to hasten pain relief in any pain crisis. A patient can go from begging to be euthanized to feeling light and liberated from an unrelenting tide of pain.

I first came in contact with children suffering from leukaemia because I used to be called in to assist with an issue entirely unrelated to pain. Back then, central venous cannulation (placing a catheter in a large vein close to the heart) was not a commonly performed procedure, and not all anaesthesiologists would do it. So, when a child needed a central venous cannulation for aggressive chemotherapy,

I would be roped in. It was then that I wandered into their world of pain for the first time. Dr Salim, the hemato-oncologist, would allow me to administer my technique of repeated small doses of injectable morphine to the children. I was not merely poking catheters into them; I became friends with these children because I was the one who could take away some of their pain and torment.

One day, I got called into the hospital at 3 a.m. in the morning. Dr Salim wanted my help with a child who had leukaemia. The boy was extremely ill and the doctor felt that as a last resort, he should try a particular chemotherapeutic agent for which I was required to do a central venous cannulation. I was hesitant considering the condition of the little boy, but I also thought it my duty to perform the procedure.

But when I approached the child, his father said, 'I will not let you touch him. There have been enough needles into him. I know he is dying; let him die in peace. Take your needles away.'

His anger and indignation had a strange effect on me. I felt a flood of relief that I would not have to do the painful cannulation for the boy, who was in an incurable condition. I assured the father that I certainly understood and had no intention to poke any more needles into his son without his consent. His anger abated a little. 'If you can,' he said softly, 'give him something for the pain. That is the least we can do for him. I can't bear the thought of him dying in suffering like this.'

With Dr Salim's permission, I started my now tried-and-trusted repetitive small dose technique. He had a bit of nausea at times, and to counter that I added an anti-emetic. I found that 3 milligrams of morphine into the vein would make him almost completely pain free for a few hours. I diluted morphine in a syringe so that every millilitre would be 3 milligrams, labelled the syringe and gave it to the nurse with instructions to give a millilitre whenever the child had pain.

Sadly, I did not know enough to give the next dose before the pain came on. It was only much later that I learnt that the subsequent dose could safely go in before the effect of the previous dose had worn off and prevent an episode of pain every few hours.

I started seeing the boy a couple of times every day. He would be quite chatty at times, talking to me about ordinary matters rather than about his disease or his pain. It made me immensely happy that I had enabled him to be in this state, to feel normal at least for a few hours. I held that warm, gratifying feeling in my heart.

A couple of days later when I visited him the little boy appeared to be very ill, but perked up enough to give me a slight smile. 'How are you?' I asked. 'I am quite okay now,' the boy said with another smile. He died an hour later. It was not sadness that took hold of me; it was fulfilment. In his inevitable passage towards death, I was able to satisfy the wish of the little boy's father that he would not go in anguish.

FOURTEEN

MY FIRST AFFAIR WITH COMMUNITY ENGAGEMENT

Dr Suresh Kumar, a young doctor who had joined the department of anaesthesiology for a two-year postgraduate course, became interested in my work with pain. After completing his routine work, he would stand beside me and observe as I performed my procedures. Suresh was curious about nerve blocks, and about how I was trying to combine the use of painkillers with my procedures. He was particularly intrigued by the fact that I was adopting the role of the patient's primary physician when they did not have a doctor treating them any more.

It was the beginning of a long-term association, and one that would stand me in good stead in my palliative care journey. I was introduced to Suresh's close friend, Asok Kumar, who ran a printing press. His only connection with medical science was that he often played the role of a Good Samaritan by helpfully accompanying relatives or friends to meet doctors when required.

It was through Asok's compassionate lens that I was clearly able to see the skewed singular focus of the medical system on diseases; how appallingly little it focused on the human being and how utterly lopsided its obsession with diagnosis was. None of us dreamed at the time that

Asok was blazing a brand-new trail in Indian healthcare, as the first palliative care volunteer. Thousands would follow in his footsteps, eventually creating one of the most successful community-based palliative care services in the world.

Suresh, Asok, and I frequently discussed caring for patients and I would often find their perspectives, which they had garnered from their own personal experiences, exceptionally thought-provoking. Suresh, for example, once told me about his friend's mother. The friend had moved to the north of the country to study for his post-graduation and Suresh was helping to look after his ailing mother. She told him, 'Suresh, you are interested only in my medicines, not in me.'

Suresh said that statement opened his eyes. It held a powerful lesson for me as well. I was already thinking a lot on those lines. What is the intent of medical science? Is it solely to diagnose and treat diseases, or should it also aim to make people feel better?

Asok had a steady stream of such stories to narrate. He felt compelled to help others in trouble, and as a result was a frequent 'bystander' when friends or family interacted with the medical system. If Asok some day writes a book on medical absurdities, it would make for invaluable reading for medical and allied healthcare professionals.

Our conversations revolved around trying to find solutions for families whose finances were in dire straits so that they could afford medicines. Most often, a solution would emerge, and it would quite frequently involve us dipping into our own pockets.

The professor's suicide following the nerve block had been a huge blow to me, striking me where it really hurt.

It also made me sit up and think. I brooded over it a great deal, yet nothing in the medical books that I had studied so far gave me any answers.

Quite accidentally, I came across a book in my cupboard. It was called *Symptom Control in Far Advanced Cancer: Pain Relief* by Robert Twycross and Sylvia Lack. I had purchased the book out of a catalogue a few years earlier when I had some money during my Oman days. I had ordered it believing it would enlighten me on nerve blocks, particularly the different kinds of nerve blocks. So you can imagine my utter disappointment to find that the book had a small, rather dismissive paragraph on the subject and I had promptly abandoned it. As it happens in life sometimes, the book presented itself to me once again, quite serendipitously, when I was of a mind to make use of it. When I opened it this time, several elements came into focus; not only possible answers to the questions raised by the professor's death, but to some bigger questions as well. It dawned on me that the book was not only about advanced cancer, it was about people with advanced cancer.

Around that time, I came to hear about a palliative care workshop being conducted in Trivandrum by Ms Gilly Burn, a British nurse. I decided to attend the workshop and came away feeling significantly enlightened. Many things that she talked about radically contradicted everything that I had studied. For instance, in my study of anaesthesiology, the one contraindication for morphine was breathlessness. Here, Gilly was introducing morphine as the treatment for breathlessness in cancer. She also talked about pain management and about people.

I was profoundly impressed. I did not get around to

talking to her at that time, perhaps because she was busy or I was too timid. A few months later, in early 1993, I heard that Gilly was back for another workshop in Trivandrum and I boarded a train from Calicut to attend it. This time she was using an interactive computer program, quite a novelty at that time. It was vastly impressive, not only because of the innovative nature of the program, but also because of Gilly's sheer dynamism.

At the end of the lecture, I plucked up the courage and went over to speak with her. I told her about the modest palliative care work that I was doing in Calicut, just an overnight train journey away. 'Do you think,' I shakily put forth, 'that at some point of time you could visit and guide us?'

'How about the day after tomorrow?' Gilly replied robustly. That was the kind of person she was. Gilly did not believe in train reservations. Instead, she would go to the railway station, barge into the station master's office, and make such a persistent nuisance of herself, I suppose, that he would somehow pull a sleeper berth out of his hat. Gilly was with us in Calicut two days later, as she had promised.

With much trepidation and a tremendous inferiority complex pushing me down (I knew that I had no proper training, and did not know if what I was doing was of any value), I showed Gilly what we did. I took her through the register in which we kept the records of our patients and she saw two or three patients that were being treated on that day. As the visit concluded after an hour, Gilly asked me, 'Would you like to go for a course in Oxford in September?'

Would I! I jumped at the chance. I had four months to secure a visa and prepare for the trip of my life.

Without anyone pointing it out in so many words, the work with Suresh and Asok taught me the value of teamwork, of how individual strengths could be shared with others to overcome the deficiency in the areas of a partner's weakness. And Gilly's involvement and contribution taught me the value of empowering oneself with adequate education while entering a new field.

FIFTEEN

THE GROUP OF SEVEN: PAIN AND PALLIATIVE CARE SOCIETY

Along with the Twycross book, Gilly's two teaching sessions, and with lessons I had gained from my patients, the basic foundation for my palliative care practice had been laid, albeit, a shaky one. The patients and their needs continued to grow steadily, more so because we were becoming aware of and sensitive to hitherto unseen requirements. One day, during one of my conversations with Suresh and Asok, I suggested we form an organization.

'Let us register a charity so that we can support the treatment of needy patients,' I said.

'Let us aim even higher,' Suresh said.

The discussion meandered in different directions and by the end of that evening, we had arrived at the decision to register a society to develop palliative care. We decided to operate in seven northern districts of Kerala to start with. Having exhausted all our combined inspiration for the day, we had trouble finding a name for it, and eventually settled on the not-too-imaginative 'Pain and Palliative Care Society'.

We needed more people to become members. We needed to build a corps of supporters and in any case, a minimum of seven members was legally required for a charitable society to be registered. Who could we enrol? Dr Molly John was an obvious choice along with Dr E. K. Ramadas, another colleague who had begun to take an interest in our work.

Several months earlier, I had made a presentation about my efforts in pain management at an academic club of professionals called the Ehrlich's Club. After the talk, Dr Ganapathi Rao, a professor of medicine, quietly said to me in the course of our conversation, 'Count me in. I will be glad to help.' And so we did, and he joined our fledgling endeavour.

Dr S. Achuthan Nair, who had many years of experience both as a cardiothoracic surgeon as well as a hospital administrator, and who I regarded as an older brother, agreed to help when I told him what we wanted to do.

Asok's inputs had taught me that having non-medical people on board is crucial. Having only doctors meant that we would run the risk of becoming an entity that would be unidimensional and clinical. The human angle needed to be infused right from the start and remain a defining touchstone.

We had all read an autobiography by a writer called Thikkodiyan. We decided to ask him to get involved, forgetting the fact that none of us had the remotest personal connection with him. We only knew him through his book, which revealed major adversities he had overcome heroically to become an eminent Malayalam writer. What drew me most to his autobiography was the fact that not once did he diminish another human being by speaking ill of any person. He also had the rare and singular gift of being able to laugh at himself.

So, off we went—Asok, Suresh, and I—to meet Thikkodiyan. I wonder what he thought of us, three completely random people that he didn't know at all, marching into his life and asking him to be a member of some crazy society. To his credit, he gave us a patient hearing and once he understood the nature of the cause, wholeheartedly agreed to become a member.

We had our magic number of seven—the founders of the Pain and Palliative Care Society (PPCS) of Calicut. We had no idea then what a difference our 'group of seven' would make in the long run.

Not that there weren't any stumbling blocks. I was in the government service and needed official permission to work outside the government system, even if it was for a charitable society. Any request would likely wind its way into the dark recesses of the government secretariat in Trivandrum, never to be seen again, or I would receive an ambiguous rejection.

Daunted by these notions, I did not immediately put in my request for permission to establish and chair the PPCS. Biding my time, I waited until a friend, the vice principal of the Calicut Medical College, briefly took office as the principal incharge for a few days. He granted me the written permission in his capacity as the head of the institution. None of us was certain of the legality or validity of that action, but we decided to move ahead with our plan.

The next step was to get permission to begin the clinical work within the medical college hospital. This time round, the fact that I was the head of department as well as a member of the college management committee helped. The committee granted us permission for the PPCS to function inside the medical college, at 'no cost to the government'.

SIXTEEN

MY UK SOJOURN

In September 1993, I found myself in the company of five other Indian doctors who had been chosen to participate in a ten-week course run by Dr Robert Twycross at Oxford. Gilly had scoured the country to identify six people who she believed could help patients in need of palliative care, and then found the money for the doctors to attend the course.

There are many things about that course that I will never forget. One was the bitter cold. It was only September, still warm by English standards, but my poor tropical bones and teeth would not stop clattering in spite of wearing every article of warm clothing in my arsenal. Another was the revelation that people had made massive advances in the kind of treatment that I was still attempting to clumsily provide. Dr Robert Twycross proved to be a teacher par excellence. What good fortune to have early lessons from such a veritable guru! And Gilly was not only a great teacher, but also a mother hen to all of us.

The first two weeks of classroom sessions were followed by placements as an observer in three different palliative care establishments: the Cynthia Spencer Hospice in Northampton, Willen Hospice in Milton Keynes, and St James's Hospital in Leeds. Shadowing Dr

John Smith in Northampton and Dr Stephen Dyer in Milton Keynes yielded eye-opening lessons.

When I had started working in palliative care in Calicut, I had not undergone any formal education in the subject. The little knowledge I had gathered had come from a book and from the workshops conducted by Gilly Burn that I had attended. But it was this course that finally took me deep enough into the science of palliative medicine and the art of compassion. This was my first meaningful formal education in palliative care. Coming from a conservative state like Kerala, I also got my first glimpse of the wide cultural dissimilarities between the UK and India.

To me, there seemed to be too many old patients lying alone on their beds in the UK hospices. True, a nurse would appear at the push of a button but once their immediate needs had been attended to, they would be alone again.

I distinctly remember a lady who had been divorced four times. The last divorce, in her own words, had been because the man had been 'too good'. She found it maddening that he was always right. That evening I reflected in my diary, 'I suppose I shall understand that in about a million years.'

Could it be that marriages in India were seemingly a little more stable than those in England because a couple whose marriage had been 'arranged' had far fewer expectations from one another, and did not extricate themselves from the arrangement even if the spouse was too good or overbearing? It must have been infuriating for that lonely lady to have her erstwhile husband correcting her all the time, but I could not imagine an Indian divorce on those grounds; at least not in those days.

I remember a conversation on end-of-life between Dr

Stephen Dyer and a ninety-two-year-old patient. The man knew he had advanced cancer. Stephen wanted to know his aspirations; what did the man hope for? The man mouthed the words, 'To live'.

Taking his time to gently navigate this highly sensitive territory, Stephen explained that his time was limited. 'John, with the remaining time you have, what do you want to do with your life?' he asked the man.

He received the same response: 'Live'.

Do people in the West have a greater wish to keep on living as compared to Indians? Does the average Indian's belief in reincarnation empower him or her to be more accepting of mortality? I can't claim to know the answer but I doubt that it does. It's not as though most Indians welcome death with open arms, though there are a few rare ones who do. My experience of the West is too limited to draw a definitive comparison, and it may well be that the man expressing a desire to live was saying that he wanted more than merely to be kept alive. I suspect he wanted to live in the fullest sense of the word—to continue to experience the full spectrum of life.

On concluding our placements as observers, we got together at the education centre at the hospice in Esher for two more weeks of interactions; this time devoted to communication skills and the not-so-medical stuff in palliative care.

SEVENTEEN

SHAPING A NEW PARADIGM

While I was expanding my horizons in the UK, Suresh and Asok were making progress with the formalities of registering the charitable society. Asok, being equipped with infinite patience, was doing a lot of the unenviable work of running around government offices. When I returned at the end of ten weeks, we had a registered charitable society on our hands, the Pain and Palliative Care Society.

Six founding members had dipped into our own pockets (most of them rather shallow) and come up with Rs 250 each, enabling us to begin with a small capital of Rs 1,500. In addition to the cost of registration, some of this money went towards buying a couple of registers and account books. I served as the official chairman, the unofficial clerk, and the incompetent accountant of the Pain and Palliative Care Society, until eventually (and thankfully) willing volunteers came forward to share this work and a few other tasks.

We decided to craft a brochure to help raise funds and create awareness about our work. The creation of the brochure was an opportunity for Asok to teach me yet another profound lesson. We could not afford a professional designer. The task of putting the brochure together was mine, resulting in an amateurish product. I remember it featured this line at the bottom: 'Victims of advanced cancer need your help; lend a hand!'

Asok was the one to immediately point out that the word 'victim' was completely inappropriate. The rhetoric of victimhood was diminishing the person afflicted with an illness. It took courage to traverse the territory of cancer or any advanced illness, and every day that they overcame, whether with difficulty or with grace and fortitude, deserved to be acknowledged as a victory. This clearly represented the major difference between the way I as a doctor viewed the disease and Asok as a human being, saw it.

One thousand five hundred rupees was not much by any standard. We were reaching into our pockets again, when Gilly fortuitously reappeared on the scene. She would spend several months at a time in India, returning to the UK to raise money for her next visit.

Gilly magnanimously gave us a cheque for one lakh rupees—an amount that was hard to wrap our heads around. It was the kind of money we had only heard of being spent on this kind of work elsewhere in the world.

It was the break we needed, and with this impetus there was no looking back. The work grew from strength to strength. Before Gilly's donation ran out, spontaneous donations had started coming in. We came to learn how supportive the community could be. We also learnt how essential it was to give visibility to our work. There is nobility in the principle, 'Do not let your left hand know what your right hand does,' but I think there is greater nobility in giving visibility to good work so that it brings in resources and support. The people who need care matter more than our own feelings of nobility.

We envisioned a multidisciplinary pain and palliative care clinic, and so I went around trying to rope in my colleagues from several disciplines. The response, all things considered, was not bad. Our first multidisciplinary pain and palliative care clinic was attended by two neurologists, an oncologist, an internist, a general surgeon, and a psychiatrist. Quite impressive! What could be better?

There was one problem, though. There were no patients. Not even one, despite the fact that we had sent circulars to several departments.

Several specialists dropped by in the following weeks, but it was becoming increasingly apparent that they could do more by referring patients in need and being available when needed, rather than just walking across to the clinic once a week. Subsequently, I approached them individually when I needed consultations for any patient. Gradually, patients started trickling in. I am still grateful to those doctors—all of whom were very busy people—for having volunteered to participate in what they saw as a novel endeavour.

After a formal permission to launch the service was extracted 'at no cost to the government', our facilities were negligible. When the single room was no longer adequate to receive and see the growing number of patients, as the head of the department, I took the liberty to use the adjoining classroom whenever it was free. The patients had to wait in the corridor.

Asok resourcefully coaxed someone to donate a couple of narrow couches to allow sick patients to lie down while they waited. They had to be narrow; or else they would block the corridor. The couches massively improved the scene outside the general outpatient department, where very weak patients regularly collapsed on the floor.

Staffing was a pervasive issue at the palliative care clinic. Suresh had qualified as an anaesthesiologist and was now employed in a private hospital. Patients had no one to receive them when they dropped in. More often than not, I would be engaged in the operation theatre. Suresh and Asok enlisted the services of their friend Meena, who had some informal nursing experience. Her daughter Nila had just started kindergarten and therefore she had some spare time in the day.

Meena must have felt alone in a world surrounded by people in pain for she persuaded her friend Lissy to join her. Lissy was in the same boat, her son Sidharth having just started school. With Asok and Suresh dropping in after their routine work in the afternoons, and Meena and Lissy helping me through the day, we had a team of sorts. It wasn't apparent to any of us at the time, but I realize now that Asok, Meena, and Lissy had started a gentle revolution. As lay members of the community, they were graciously and spontaneously accepting that they had a responsibility to their fellow human beings in suffering. And, they were coming forward to do something about it. It was uncharted territory and, I imagine, not always easy for these pioneers.

I silently admired their spirit. They persevered; they would show up every day, armed with the little knowledge I had shared with them and their personal wisdom, and they would listen to patients. Considering that my own palliative care knowledge had huge gaps at that stage, what I imparted to them must have been woefully inadequate. But we were companions on a journey mentoring each other across a sharp learning curve.

The community was receptive to our efforts and the media offered its support. Colleagues, however, found it harder to get on board with this new paradigm. The old aphorism goes: 'First they ignore you, then they laugh at you, then they fight you, and then you win.' We experienced those stages intimately, but in the background we also had many encouraging colleagues whose reassuring presence helped us survive and progress. We moved forward at a painstakingly slow pace.

International support validated us and served to provide us credibility and, very importantly, education. Dr Robert Twycross would visit twice a year and spend weeks teaching and mentoring. Gilly persuaded Dr Jan Stjernswärd, the then chief of cancer and palliative care at the WHO to visit. With a single stroke of his pen, he declared us as a WHO demonstration project. We were delighted.

Val Hunkin, a British nurse, started accompanying Dr Robert Twycross to teach communication skills. Her lessons were inestimable and helped change lives all over India for many years, till eventually she sadly succumbed to cancer.

Besides imparting communication skills, Val brought Bruce Davis, a retired businessman and philanthropist in Cornwall into our fold. She got him to take an interest in us, and through the Wilfrid Bruce Davis Trust, he began extending financial assistance to us. 'Saintly' is the word that springs to my mind when I think of Bruce. He went on to pay for the construction of the Institute of Palliative Medicine (IPM) in Calicut, the first of many projects he funded in the ensuing years.

Today, a vital part of our palliative care centre at Trivandrum (Thiruvananthapuram) is our training centre, which has been named the Bruce Davis Training Centre. He was a cherished friend, well-wisher, and guide to several palliative care institutions and to Pallium India. From him and from the numerous people who helped us from around the world, I learnt that we are all citizens of one world. By being open to learning and accepting constructive criticism and support, we can grow to heights that small teams cocooned in their own limited spheres may not have the opportunity to.

We could not have achieved what we did unless we had the support of the community around us. The example demonstrated by Asok, Meena, and Lissy came to be followed in every palliative care centre that we catalysed and community participation became the hallmark of palliative care delivery in Kerala. Later, Suresh gave structure to it as the Neighbourhood Network in Palliative Care (NNPC) and the movement inspired compassionate communities elsewhere too.

EIGHTEEN

ON THE ORAL MORPHINE TRAIL

While oral morphine was hard to come by, we had access to injectable morphine and pethidine at our palliative care clinic in Calicut. There were frequent interruptions in the supply of these precious commodities, but I had commendable nagging abilities and by constantly hounding the powers that be, I was able to ensure the availability of at least one drug, if not both.

I was aware that these injections had been rather easily available some fifteen to twenty years earlier. Back in the time when I was a house surgeon, I could simply write out a prescription in duplicate, sign it myself and the patient could buy it at any pharmacy. Something had changed drastically since then. It was the introduction of the draconian Narcotic Drugs and Psychotropic Substances (NDPS) Act of 1985, a law that had significantly worsened the pain burden in India since its inception.

These injections also didn't quite cut it when it came to sustained pain relief. When somebody came into my clinic doubled over in pain, the injections I administered served to reduce some of their anguish for the time being, but patients had to go home at some point. A new pattern, a problematic one, began to emerge—people were refusing to leave the hospital. This was in turn beginning to annoy physicians and surgeons who desperately needed the beds to be freed up for new patients seeking admission.

The solution was clear as day—we needed oral morphine. The drug controller had categorically refused to introduce another 'addictive' drug into the state. The pain clinic at the Regional Cancer Centre in Trivandrum had oral morphine; and that was all.

With no other choice, I turned to the cancer centre. We received one consignment thanks to the kind director. Although the relief was temporary, it was a palpable one. We could send patients home with the morphine. But when the time came to procure the next batch, the centre could not give us any more.

We had no other recourse, and the time had come for us to get our own licences. I did not know it then; but this effort would throw me headlong into a maze of bureaucratic tangles I didn't know existed.

I discovered that we needed three licences, all of them to be valid at the same time. Being in Kerala was lucky, I was told; most states demanded four licences.

Let me try and break down this labyrinth for you: first, we needed a possession licence that would specify not only the quantity that we could possess at any given point in time, but also the particular formulation mentioned on the licence. This meant that if the licence mentioned tablets, I could not possess morphine syrup. To obtain this licence, I had to go to the excise inspector's office in my own city and apply. But, the application process itself was a big mystery—we did not know, for example, whom to address the application to, or where to find the prescribed application.

After a fair bit of dogged effort, we found it, and as

always Asok went after it. With his matchless powers of persuasion, he managed to convince the excise inspector that neither he nor I was a drug peddler trying to procure morphine to sell it on the street to make money, no matter how much we may have looked the part at the time. The inspector came and 'inspected' our institution. I didn't exactly understand what he was looking for. Neither did he, in my opinion. That was the procedure—he had to visit. For equally unfathomable reasons, he made the recommendation to the excise commissioner's office in Trivandrum.

'How long will it take?' I asked. He couldn't say.

'But I will get it, won't I?' I persisted.

'Not sure', he said. 'Not unless you go and convince the excise secretary in Trivandrum.'

So off I went to meet the secretary. It was a twelve-hour overnight train journey to the state capital. Once I got there, he made me wait for four hours. I was just one of the many people who came to him for licences, particularly for alcohol for medicinal use, which was commonly believed to be diverted to make illicit liquor.

Four hours in a government office corridor is a long time. But I had made up my mind; now that I had come all this way, I was going to see him. He eventually let me in and softened a little when I explained the problem to him and agreed to do what was needed to help me. The 'needful' as we say in India, unfortunately, was just putting me through to the drug controller for his concurrence. So off I went to the drug controller's office.

The drug controller was reputedly a very upright person. He refused outright. He did not want a society corrupted by illicit drugs. I tried to explain to him how we could use it safely but was abruptly stopped. I went back home, tail between my legs.

A few months later, the tide turned in our favour when a new excise secretary assumed office. He was Dr Venu, a medical doctor, a former student of our medical college, who had given up being a doctor and had gone into administrative service. He heard my story and called the drug controller over the phone.

'My professor will be coming to you for a recommendation on our query about his application for oral morphine. He should have your letter of approval in his pocket within half an hour,' he instructed in rather clipped tones.

I was gobsmacked! I had never ever seen this kind of functioning in a government office. I found myself before a bristling drug controller, who honestly believed that he was being pressurised into doing something that was morally distasteful and wrong. And, by signing off on such a document, he would be held responsible for the scourge being unleashed on a respectable society.

I decided that the prudent thing to do would be to stay silent, and came back with the required letter, which felt like hot coal in my pocket. I eventually got the possession licence along with an import permit with which I could order the medicine from Ahmedabad. There was quite a bit of money to be paid, which we raised through what can only be called plain and simple begging.

Now the supplier in Ahmedabad had to procure an export permit. And then they had to send the morphine by registered post. We had to receive this consignment before the validity of the two permits expired. The same process had to be repeated every single time. The possession licence had to be renewed every year and for every consignment, we needed an import permit, and the supplier needed an export permit. It was an exasperating and exhausting cycle, pockmarked and botched by hindrances and incompetence, but the interminable hours endured in government corridors were worth the relief of getting our hands on oral morphine.

All our sweat and frustrations paled into insignificance, when we saw the smiles on the faces of our patients; there were smiles even on faces marred by advanced cancer. This led to more conversation and more stories tumbling out from our patients after their pain was assuaged. Patients could now hold Meena's hand and tell her how much they had endured, how much they appreciated our care, or hug Lissy and thank her. And once they opened up, the torrent of stories swept us upward, and we began learning from them. We learnt how all-consuming pain can be, and how it can leave humans with no space to be human, and how dramatically they can become human again once their pain reduces in reasonable time.

NINETEEN

NAVIGATING INDIAN BUREAUCRACY

I am grateful to providence for bringing several people into my life. One of them has to be David Joranson, an American of Swedish descent, who had a profound impact in my life. I shall always remember our first meeting at Oxford in 1995. We met at a working committee meeting that Dr Robert Twycross had invited me to. I remember the sunken seating area outside the conference hall, where David sought me out. He was looking for an Indian partner to work with to make opioids available in India.

David's career had been an interesting one. He had worked as a seaman in a submarine for several years. Later, he became a drug regulator and became interested in the global burden of pain and the inequity in access to opioid medicines like morphine. Eventually, he set up the Pain and Policy Studies Group (PPSG) at the University of Madison-Wisconsin in USA and started working with governments all over the world to analyse their laws and policies governing access to opioid medicines.

Till I met David, I had not even heard that a stream of study called policy analysis existed. David's deep commitment to his work was always laced with a great sense of humour. Maybe, being cooped up in a submarine for long periods of time had taught him enough patience to deal with the infamous bureaucracy of developing countries.

When I met him, David had already made contact with several key people in India—Romesh Bhattacharji, the narcotics commissioner in the 1990s, and M. C. Mehanathan, the director of narcotics in the Department of Revenue. This was when I started my tryst with the revenue department of the Government of India.

David held my hand and guided me on working with governments. He even found the money for my travel to Delhi. I would check in at the YWCA family hostel in Delhi; while he would find a hotel not far from it, and we worked together through days and evenings, often late into the night. We would meet everyone who mattered; his calling card as the director of a WHO collaborating centre opened doors on which I would have had no hope of even knocking.

Around this time, a pharmacologist in Delhi, Dr Ravindra Ghooi, found himself in the shoes of a son worrying about his mother's cancer. What if she developed pain? Three-fourths of all people with cancer get pain at one time or other. And she was in India where morphine was out of reach for most!

Curiously, he found people who would help him procure it on the sly; but not legally. What about people who did not have his kind of connections? He decided to approach the court to remedy this violation of human right to life with dignity.

Curiously, he found that it was not easy to prove to the court that there was a problem. He approached doctors dealing with pain management. They did not want to get involved in legal hassles or to annoy government officials.

After his mother's death, he connected with us, wishing to seek a solution to this problem for people in pain. David and I worked with him to arm him with enough facts and documents to approach the High Court of Delhi. It took more than a year, but eventually the case came up for a final hearing.

'What do you want?' the court asked.

'We want morphine to be available to those who need it for pain relief,' the lawyer responded.

The court ordered in his favour and asked the government to ensure speedy access to morphine for those who needed it for pain relief.

We all realized later that the request should have been more specific, and should have spelt out the measures needed to access opioids and to provide pain relief. As it turned out, the order was a bit vague, like 'let there be morphine'; nevertheless, it was a success and the court order turned out to be an agent of change for the future.

Gilly had convinced Dr Yusuf Hamied, the head of Cipla Pharmaceuticals, to manufacture low-cost oral morphine. Dr Hamied is a person that the world should be thankful for—a man who was responsible for defying the profit worshippers and for bringing low-cost antiretroviral medicines to the poorer parts of the world, including sub-Saharan Africa. Would the world today have been the same without that one important step? Well, he set a benchmark by giving us morphine at less than one rupee for a 10-milligram tablet.

In the meantime, David, with his colleagues and us, had prepared a draft law seeking to amend the NDPS Act. The Department of Revenue decided that changing the law would be too cumbersome a process and instead decided to ask all states to change their rules. Working from the basic draft provided by David, the Department of Revenue created some model rules and in 1998 asked all states to modify their rules following the model.

I sat back and waited for the states to follow the instructions. Except for three states, none followed the central government's instruction; they were not legally obligated to do so. Interestingly, the three states which spontaneously changed the rules following the central government's instruction did not really need to, yet; there was little palliative care happening there.

David and I started travelling state by state, often with one of David's colleagues and one of mine. We would work with a palliative care champion in the state, who would do the legwork of getting people together, including the senior officials and sometimes a minister. There were some successes and some failures.

Kerala was certainly a success. Enough background work had been done by then. Palliative care was a known entity in Kerala. But all this work would have been meaningless if we were not able to convert it into actual patient care and to make it visible.

As our work grew, we gained some expertise, and our patients continued teaching us.

DEPTHS OF SUFFERING; HEIGHTS OF RELIEF

If I can stop one heart from breaking,
I shall not live in vain;
If I can ease one life the aching,
Or cool one pain,
Or help one fainting robin
Unto his nest again,
I shall not live in vain.

—Emily Dickinson[*]

---

[*]Emily Dickinson, 'If I Can Stop One Heart from Breaking', *Poems by Emily Dickinson*, Mabel Loomis Todd and T. W. Higginson (eds.), Boston: Little, Brown, & Company, 1800.

TWENTY

CHILDREN NEED ANSWERS

Children are amazingly resilient. In my experience, they can process bad news much more easily than adults. Of course, this is not true for all children, or for all adults for that matter; this is but a generalization that applies to the majority. We completely fail to recognize children's reasoning abilities. 'After all,' we say, 'he is but a child. What can he understand?'

When we adults fail to give children vital information, they suffer. They suffer terribly. When we hide information, they sense it and immediately get the message that questions are pointless. And if they suspect we are covering something up, they can get extremely anxious.

In one of the hospitals I worked in, we tried to prevent 'procedure-related pain' in children suffering from cancer. Until we intervened, the situation had been pathetic. Doctors and nurses at varying levels of training and with varying expertise would perform venepuncture—the insertion of a cannula into a vein for intravenous administration of medicines. Often, the child would be held down by force.

Bone marrow puncture is a procedure where a thick, large needle goes directly into the bone to draw out blood cells from the centre of the bone. It is often done with no attempt at all to prevent or treat the ensuing pain. (The covering of the bone, periosteum, is one of the most sensitive parts of the body, and a needle going through it can cause terrible pain.) The same holds true for lumbar punctures where the heftiest hospital attendants would tear the child away from their mother's arms and almost break the child in two to keep the back curved while a needle was inserted between the two vertebrae.

Such pain impacts much more than physical suffering. It can cause uncontrollable panic attacks or behavioural problems in the long term. The saddest part is that much of this suffering is unnecessary. Even with limited resources, pain can be prevented.

So, to begin with, we drew up concise guidelines to prevent procedure-related pain. It was not a success. Doctors were pressed for time; they did not even want to look at it. Nurses were even busier. First attempt: failure.

We changed our strategy. Could the children be sent to our clinic prior to the procedure so that we could prepare them for a painful procedure? This worked. The little ones walked over to the clinic from the children's hospital situated across the road. It became something like a get-together, almost like playtime. We would apply EMLA cream on the skin and cover the area with a piece of sticking plaster. (EMLA is eutectic mixture of local anaesthetics, a name so long and unpronounceable that it might have been invented to bolster reverence for the medical profession.) After about forty-five minutes, these areas would become insensitive. The children would then stream back to their cancer ward for their injections.

The difference it made was phenomenal. Much of the

agony was abated; but not all.

We tweaked our methods based on feedback from the children. We had applied the cream on one spot for Abdul's lumbar puncture. Abdul was a talkative and forthright child. We asked him, 'Was it any better this time?'

'Oh, pinne!' (A sarcastic 'yes, indeed!') 'You put it on one place but they poked elsewhere.'

So, we became more liberal with the cream.

This ritual actually brought the children and their mothers closer to us. At first, only a small number of children with pain or other serious symptoms would come to us. Soon, they would all troop into our clinic. Their problems became ours. Thankfully, many paediatricians were supportive.

That was how we came to know about Abdul's fears. He had questions that nobody would answer. After our conversations with him, he understood that his cancer was curable. But he had other fears inside him.

'Ok, my cancer may be cured,' he said, 'but if not?'

'If not...?' I gently prodded and waited for him to continue.

'If I die, won't I get punished by God?' the tentative question came out in a soft voice.

'Why, Abdul?' I asked. 'Why would God punish you?'

'Because I have sinned,' was his reply.

So here was Abdul, a sinner at the age of eight or nine. What was the sin? He had often pulled his sister's hair when he was angry. He had gone once so far as to steal her pen and hide it. Wouldn't God punish him?

We called his parents in and talked about the need for an open conversation, so that the child does not harbour such unrealistic fears. His father could easily solve the problem.

He worked in a mosque.

He told us, 'For wrongs committed by children below fourteen years,' (or fifteen, I do not remember) 'they are not punished.'

That reassured Abdul. If it came to the worst, he would die. He was ready to die so long as there was no punishment in store for him.

Time and again, we came across a lot of suffering stemming from religious beliefs. Children's faith in God is often absolute. When they believe in God and in their religion, they do not doubt Him. They do not doubt their parents or other elders as well, when they give faith-based information. So, we tried our best to help children overcome some irrational fears.

Little Joseph was another child in misery because of fears associated with death.

One day, Joseph's mother rushed into our clinic, and started sobbing uncontrollably. A few minutes later, having cried her heart out, she explained that she had come in just to cry.

'Mom, will I die before you?' her son had asked her that day.

The question was overwhelming. She asked the mother in the next bed to look after the boy for a while and rushed to us, where she felt safe to cry, and where she could be sure of a shoulder to cry on, or a hand to hold hers.

By this time, we were more or less familiar with the fears that children with terminal illness often lived with. They had their own social circle in the ward for discussions. The mothers would try to keep secrets from them; and so would the nurses and doctors. In their foolish faith in the assumed stupidity of children, adults think kids will never know. But the kids would talk to one another when their mothers were out of earshot.

'Did you know Ram died last night? Was it C. M. L.?'
'No, A. L. L.'

The children knew the diagnoses; they knew the names, chronic myeloid leukaemia, acute lymphocytic leukaemia, and so on. They would converse, in whispers, about death.

Joseph had obviously his own concerns about death. We gently persuaded his mother to bring him to us. He might have fears, and they could be worse than reality. We needed to find out what they were in order to ease them.

After some persuasion, Joseph's mother brought him to us. I made him sit beside me and requested his mother to let me talk to him alone. She reluctantly went outside. There are some advantages to being bald, grey, and old; young people find it difficult to refuse you when you ask for a favour. Joseph's mother walked out of the room; but I could see her sari blowing in the wind against the door.

'Hey, Joseph,' I said, 'I hear you have been asking questions about death. Ask me. I shall try to answer them.'

There was no reluctance; no hesitation.

'When they bury me, won't I suffocate?' his voice turned shaky.

I could easily dispel this fear for him. No; I assured him that if he did die, there would be no suffocation because there was no discomfort at all once someone was dead. We also talked about the chances of cure for his cancer.

'Any other questions?' I asked.

'Can I go and look at that computer?' he asked. He had moved on to the next thing.

Children have short attention spans. They don't want lectures; they ask straight questions and want straight answers. That is enough to reassure them. They need to be given the opportunity to ask those intense, and at times profound, questions. Without honest answers, their misery and loneliness cannot be imagined by you or me.

Sometimes, kids may nurture unresolved anger and resentment, which will impact those around them. Then, there is no closure for the patient or the family—and that's my next story.

TWENTY-ONE

ADIEU, IN ANGER

Robin was an angry fifteen-year-old girl with whom I had built a bond.

When I first met Robin in her room, I could see that she was angry with her parents. But she opened up to me and told me all about her illness, including the type of leukaemia she had.

She was in severe pain. Though she dreaded needles, she allowed me to sit beside her and administer small doses of fentanyl, which I did with the tiniest butterfly needle. In about fifteen minutes, the pain was all but gone. Robin seemed eager to talk and in no time, I heard the reason for her anger.

When she was eleven, her father got a good job offer abroad. Not wanting to compromise on Robin's education, he had sent her to a boarding school, while her younger sister accompanied the parents. Robin found herself alone, and in angst. She hated every moment in the boarding school.

Robin's anger affected her school life. She was not easy to make friends with and was hounded by the school bully. She would spend her holidays with her parents every year, but had turned hostile towards them and her sister.

Three years later, her father received a call from the

school, asking him to take the child to a specialist as she had recurrent fevers, and something was not right.

The father took Robin from the local hospital to a tertiary hospital, eventually to get a diagnosis of leukaemia. The devastated family decided to return to India.

'That was what he was worried about,' Robin told me, 'About losing his job and money. He was not really worried about me or my disease, though he was the reason for it.'

'Why do you say he was the reason for the disease?' I asked Robin gently.

'I would not have got it, if he had not sent me to that boarding school. That's what gave me the disease.'

The father could afford to provide any treatment to Robin that her oncologist recommended, and she certainly got a lot of it.

Robin, however, did not do well with chemotherapy. Even the words 'chemotherapy', 'drip', or 'cannula' would cause her great anguish and lead her to retch uncontrollably. No wonder she found it difficult to accept my needle, however tiny, and I could very well see that it was not easy for her. Eventually, the prospect of pain relief did the trick. She would shut her eyes tight and clench her teeth to accept a butterfly needle and a syringe, but not an infusion set or an intravenous cannula, let alone chemotherapy.

How could the father cope with her pent-up anger? I wondered.

'She is just a child, isn't she? She will be happy when she gets better,' he would say philosophically.

The miracle of pain relief made me Robin's closest friend in the hospital. She would ask to see me many times, and I had to do home visits several times a week on her bidding.

I never got to talk much with her mother. The otherwise progressive household seemed to be old-fashioned about women. When I asked to talk with her mother, she would appear behind the door, half hidden by the curtain. I don't think I ever got to see her face completely.

But the little that I saw told me that she was possibly suffering much more than the father. The father seemed to laugh the child's anger off. The mother was vulnerable and bore the full brunt of Robin's anger. Robin would pick up objects and throw them at her mother, or strike out with her arms and hurt her. I thought I might get Robin to look at her own anger with a different perspective over a few days of conversation.

But I never succeeded. The parents possibly did not like the fact that Robin was disclosing family secrets to me. I got a clear instruction; my home visits were no longer required. They would send a messenger for the morphine, which Robin needed. Any adjustment of medication or dose would be made based on a phone call from the family, not from the girl.

Robin is no longer alive. But I often wonder about her parents. Was the father just putting on a facade? Both the parents must have been very lonely through it all. They must have found it so difficult to accept their daughter's anger, and her eventual parting in anger.

The loss of a loved one is always difficult, but it is harder when one has to live with dreadful memories and even guilt. Especially, when the anger and suffering overshadow any beautiful thoughts to remember the person by.

TWENTY-TWO

HOPE LOST; HOPE REGAINED

If some pass on with anger in their hearts, there are some others who spread love and joy around them in the brief time they are with us. This is story of a brave young girl whose sweet but painful memory will always be with us.

Eleven-year-old Thasleena was one of our patients in Calicut in the early years of our palliative care work. We had learnt a lot from our patients and families. Thasleena possibly taught us more than most about love, endurance, courage, hope, and, above all, the fragility of life.

Thasleena was a picture of sorrow. She had a huge swelling in her thigh bone; and she found it impossible to walk. The swelling confined her to a bed or a chair. It was a cancer, and the doctors had advised amputation of the leg. The family was told that a cure was unlikely.

Thasleena refused to undergo the amputation because she did not want to be half a person. Though shattered by her decision, the parents consented. She was writhing in pain when we first saw her. With our medication, the pain was gone and then the real Thasleena emerged, one who would light up an entire room with a smile. She was never too chatty, but when she did talk, it was not only about herself, her family, and her disease. She would ask questions about every patient coming into our clinic.

In those days, we did not have huge numbers; and often patients and families became friends with one another. A community eventually evolved and Thasleena certainly was a much-loved member of that community. She felt very close to two of our most senior volunteers: Meena and Lissy.

Thasleena talked easily with everyone. She would ask me questions like 'What is going to happen to me?' We did talk about death. She asked a couple of questions and accepted my truthful answers. She did not want to dwell too much on it. Were there fears inside her? I was happy to leave it to her to decide the agenda of our conversations.

The swelling in her thigh grew. It came to a stage where she could not even turn to one side. The huge, ugly thing was weighing her down. We really thought an amputation was the only way to improve her quality of life.

At that time, the movie *Mayuri*, based on a real-life story, was being talked about a lot in the media. The film's protagonist Sudha Chandran, a young vivacious actor, had lost a leg in an accident. She not only led a normal life with the aid of an artificial limb but had also started dancing. Her dance was spectacular; the movie was truly inspiring.

During one of our heart-to-heart talks, I brought up the question of amputation again to Thasleena. It was painful for her to talk about it. It hurt me too to bring it up with her, but this is what we have to do in palliative care.

That was one of the few occasions when Thasleena sobbed uncontrollably. The thought of living with just one leg was unbearable to her. I brought up the *Mayuri* movie and Sudha Chandran's story soon inspired her. She watched the movie at home and the next day, she was ready for the amputation. The power of cinema!

The preoperative check-up showed that Thasleena already had metastatic cancer in her lungs. The family, for once, decided to hide the truth from her.

Following the surgery by a kind surgeon, Dr P. Rajan, she had a good spell for a few months. She had learnt to manage quite well on crutches. Her mother would narrate to us at the clinic the story of how Thasleena would always offer to go to the store to buy provisions and charge an ice cream for each trip. I wondered what she enjoyed more—the trip to the store on her crutches or the ice cream.

At that time, since our work was very much in the public eye, some engineers in the Public Works Department took the initiative to convert an old cellar into a palliative care clinic for us. The formal opening was attended by many dignitaries including Dr Jan Stjernswärd, the WHO's chief of cancer and palliative care, and Ms Gilly Burn, the palliative care pioneer. But the chief guest of the event was none other than Thasleena. As on all festive occasions, she had nagged her mother to get her a string of jasmines to adorn her hair. There was deafening applause as she made her way to the podium on her crutches and cut the ribbon to formally inaugurate the clinic.

By then, Thasleena was nursing a dream to walk again with an artificial limb.

Unfortunately, destiny had other plans for her. The cancer that had spread to her lungs resulted in a rather unusual complication. Periodically, she would get spontaneous pneumothorax (a collection of air between her lungs and the chest wall) that would cause intense breathlessness. She would be hospitalized and a tube inserted into her chest. The pneumothorax would cause several days of trouble before it eventually resolved.

Finally, during one of those episodes of breathlessness, she wanted to be brought to our clinic. The family thought it would be better for her to go to a nearby hospital to get emergency treatment; but Thasleena was adamant. On her way to our clinic, while gasping for air she asked, 'Are we there?' But before she got to us, she died.

In those early days of our palliative care education, this eleven-year-old 'guru' taught us lessons in resilience, acceptance, and endurance. She taught us how one can enjoy life even when in pain and with death staring one in the face.

TWENTY-THREE

A BOX OF TREASURES

People working in palliative care are often amazed by the sheer resilience and adaptive nature of children in pain. Take the case of the three-and-half-year-old Nadira. At that age, she had to deal not just with a cruel cancer in her kidney but a harsh and disruptive treatment as well. It was not easy for her but the treatment was necessary because it kept her tumour from growing, for a while at least.

Her father and mother would bring her by bus to the big hospital. About a mile away, Nadira would sense from the changing landscape that she was nearing danger zone and would start screaming. It would take the parents their combined effort and strength to carry her into the ward for chemotherapy. Once in there, she would be brutally plucked from the arms of her parents. Two or more able-bodied attendants would hold her to make her arm immobile while an injection was given. Eventually, the parents decided and the doctors concurred: no more chemotherapy. She would receive palliative care, instead. But the problem was that we were in the same campus as the hospital campus that always filled Nadira with terror. How were we to tackle this?

One of our volunteers showed us how. Nadira loved playing with dolls, so the volunteer created a doll out of a coconut shell and gave it to her to play with during her visits. Nadira fell in love with the new doll. So long as the visit was confined to our clinic, she was no longer afraid.

I was privileged that Nadira took a fancy to me. I felt so proud. If she had a choice, she would pick me to play with her. Part of the reason was perhaps that I had a toy which she liked—my stethoscope—and I would let her play with it. She liked to play doctor and I would be the patient. When colleagues assembled around to watch, she would be really excited. She would examine me and turn around to give explanations to the spectators, as if they were my family members.

My colleagues loved it when she put the stethoscope to my head, listened gravely, and proclaimed, 'Your problem is in your head.'

Yet, halfway through the game, she would often double up in pain, pressing her knees and arms to her belly, and cry violently. Her pain was by no means continuous, and that made it harder to treat. Eventually, we found a combination of medicines that reduced the intensity of her pain paroxysms.

But whether the pain was severe or not, the moment the attack subsided, she would act as if nothing had happened. She would spring up again, clutch the stethoscope, and start playing doctor. Perhaps, it was her way of adaptation. Nadira did not live long. But she left behind warm memories. I am grateful to her for considering me her friend.

We palliative care providers are often handed invaluable treasures: the memory of a kiss from a child whose pain we soothed; a loving message from someone who once attempted to end their life and then learned to love life and remain with us; a message of gratitude from the loved one of someone whose final journey we made easier.

There is this box of treasures which I store safely within me, and add to each time I am given another gift of love, joy, and wonder. And on days when I find myself asking 'What has been the meaning of my life?' it is this box I open quietly, within which lie a hundred different radiant answers.

TWENTY-FOUR

PAIN THAT FILLS LIFE

Pain is not only suffering; it clouds your mind and renders it incapable of thinking straight. It can be all-consuming, occupying every inch of your mind space.

Let me narrate Shambhu's story. At thirty-five, happy-go-lucky Shambhu was in a bad road traffic accident. He had multiple fractures in the bones around his eyes, nose, and the rest of his face. Several bones in his chest were broken and his hip was dislocated. His face was mangled beyond recognition. Broken bones and swelling had blocked his air passage. He was referred to our tertiary care hospital with the best of facilities for maxillofacial surgery.

He was unable to breathe when he arrived, but the hospital solved the breathing problem. The anaesthetist inserted a tube through his voice box into his windpipe. Though painful, it allowed him to breathe. Later, they performed a tracheotomy and made a slit in his throat, removed the other tube and instead put one straight into his windpipe through his neck.

Medically, the worst crisis had been averted. Now the doctors could work on the broken bones and the mangled face by performing elaborate reconstructive surgery. But, Shambhu was in the throes of agonizing pain, which was worst in the head and neck. Every now and then he would feel sudden stabs of intense sharp pain down his chest, and frequently a sensation of something hitting his innards, which was later identified as the suctioning of his trachea.

Coming on top of the pain, the torture inflicted by the suction catheter was unbearable to him. Shambhu felt his head would explode each time the nurse withdrew the catheter with a gentle continual twist. Gentle for her, but agonizing for him. Each twist felt like a knife going into his body and being twisted inside. After the first few insertions of the catheter, things became so bad that he would start flailing about and reacting violently whenever he saw a nurse approaching him.

The doctors wanted his permission for surgery; but he refused. He was just a live mass of pain. He could not listen to reason or think straight. He tried to indicate his refusal by shaking his head but because he was in so much pain, he couldn't do even that. In his frustration he tried to pull his intravenous lines out. So, they tied up his arms. People around him were focusing on the surgery that would set everything right and so none bothered enough about the pain that he was suffering right then. He felt alone in a world of pain, as he described later.

They came again to reason with him the next morning, untied one wrist, gave him a pad and a pen and asked him for permission for surgery again. The family was willing to give consent on his behalf. But this was not legally and ethically acceptable because he was in full possession of his faculties—in technical terms, he was competent to take the decision.

The pain had changed Shambhu from a jovial, rational, loving person to a violent, inconsiderate, and irrational person fighting everyone who was trying to help him. Repeated attempts at getting his consent for surgery failed.

Luckily, our palliative team got involved since his brother-in-law was a palliative care physician, and understood the vicious power of pain. With the surgeon's permission, we treated his pain fairly easily. Despite its possible adverse effects, we decided to use a non-steroidal, anti-inflammatory medicine after checking that he was well hydrated and his kidneys were functioning well. Subsequently, we gave him small aliquots of morphine every ten minutes.

In an hour, an amazing transformation occurred. He became Shambhu again, the person that he had been till the accident. He asked questions using his writing pad, got the information that he needed, and readily consented to surgery. Later, he said the pain relief enabled him to think straight. It gave him enormous confidence and made him feel naturally in command, with the strength to endure anything now.

In a few weeks, he walked out of the hospital, almost feeling like his old self.

Most people, including many medical and nursing professionals in India, fail to realize the depth and nature of pain. It can be beyond the average person's imagination. If severe, it affects your personality and changes you from a sociable human being to a selfish being, caring about nothing other than one's own pain. It fills the mind space, leaving no space for rational decision-making.

This change in behaviour is immediate when a sudden agonizing pain occurs, but generally resolves completely when the pain is relieved. Sadly, and more tragically, long-term pain such as low back pain often irrevocably changes a person. The person may manage to put up a normal front to the world at large, but once back in the privacy of his or her home, the facade crumbles. The irritability surprises others; and at some point, it wrecks relationships—between spouses, between parents and children, and eventually with colleagues too.

Whether pain is short term or long term, people in pain and their families desperately need help. In case of chronic pain, relief may not be complete. They need help not only to treat the pain as well as possible, but also to live with any residual pain. Even if adequately skilled support from a multidisciplinary team is not possible, we are able to make a lot of difference by facilitating family meetings and open communication.

TWENTY-FIVE

MANY FALL BETWEEN THE CRACKS

If you have stayed with me so far on my journey, you might be taken aback by all the pain and sorrow we encounter on a daily basis. We interact with grief and death at such close quarters. How do we handle it? Yes, a few people working in palliative care cannot cope with so much suffering. They burn out and leave. A few others cannot bear the close proximity to death. They leave too. Most of us stay on and enjoy doing it. How do we carry on? Especially on occasions when we fail to help our patients? Like in the case of Venu, a construction worker.

Venu's legs were paralysed when he fell at the construction site where he had been working. The fall broke his spine.

Fate had been really cruel to him. He had no sensation in his legs. If you touched or pinched them, he would feel nothing; but they were painful, nevertheless. That's the sort of joke that the nervous system sometimes plays on hapless humans. The injury in the spinal cord or in the brain could trigger painful impulses. The pain will be perceived in those areas where the part of the nervous system is supposed to subserve. It is similar to what happens sometimes to people who have had strokes and are paralysed on one side of the body.

Eventually, once our palliative care service found him, he received fortnightly visits by our team. He did not have to go to a hospital to change the catheter necessary to drain his urine; our palliative care nurse did it for him in his home. He also received medications which gave him some pain relief. If he had lived closer to our service, perhaps we could have done more. Maybe, we could have taught him some skills with which he could have earned an income, however small. That would perhaps have stopped his wife from cursing him endlessly. But he lived too far away; and we did not reach him often enough. That is all we could do, we had decided.

But our best was obviously not good enough for Venu. He might have been clinically depressed, which we might have missed, or life simply became too much of a burden for him.

One day, when his wife returned from work she saw Venu sitting up in his bed, deathly pale. He had brutally slashed his legs with a knife, and though the bone was still intact, the flesh was a mangled mess. He had lost a lot of blood. If it was any consolation to anyone, those were his paralysed limbs in which a knife could cause no pain.

His wife's screams brought the neighbours over. They bundled him into an ambulance and sent him to the hospital. He had figured that because his legs had no sensation, he could hack them up and he would die.

But he did not. The medical system which had hardly cared during his many years of suffering now sprang into action. Here was something they could handle: loss of blood and low blood pressure. All its forces were brought to bear on him. There was a mad scramble for blood; a couple of cursing cousins (reluctantly) and caring strangers (willingly) donated blood. Surgery and many weeks of suffering followed.

Eventually, he was sent home with a wound that had not healed and several bad pressure sores on his back.

The police had filed a criminal case against him. Suicide was illegal in India until 2017. So here he was, a criminal receiving court notices and police visits.

Once he returned home, his wife continued her cursing. Eventually, Venu died.

I know we did our best for Venu. His life was miserable, but it might have been worse if we had not given him some love, companionship, and care. Our volunteers and staff were able to alleviate his insufferable loneliness and pain in a small way. He could take shelter in their understanding and kindness for a while. But we had also failed to take him out of his hell; it is tough to reconcile with failure.

Sometimes, the system also lets us down and makes it difficult for us to help people. For example, this happens whenever there is a bandh or a hartal in Kerala, an extreme form of a general strike, when life as usual comes to a halt. Unfortunately, during a bandh, when the state becomes paralysed, and transport is disrupted, people are scared to come out on the roads. When such strikes are sudden and untargeted, it is the poor who are affected most, and when the protest prevents someone who is ill from receiving treatment, this results in the worst kind of cruelty.

As a doctor working in the government hospital, time and again, I have seen the cruel consequences on patients. When a bandh is announced without warning, a patient waiting in the hospital for a month for surgery is told that the operating theatre will not function. The hospital is paralysed because of the strike. Even if they want to, most of the staff cannot report to work.

As an anaesthesiologist, one of my worst memories has been standing at the head of an operating table and watching a young woman bleed to death after a caesarean. She needed more than a litre of blood and we could not get anyone to come to the hospital and donate blood.

Her baby survived.

Every single strike paralyses palliative home visits all over the state, even to this day. As many as 900-odd palliative care nurses, one in each panchayat, following the implementation of the Kerala government palliative care policy,[*] are forced to stay home while the patients who they were supposed to visit are left high and dry.

I can never forget Thankaiyan. In the week following a hartal, he held on to my hand and begged me to euthanize him. He had suffered immensely during the strike, having run out of his crucial pain medicines.

It is during these times that working in palliative care can become unbearable, and one can feel overwhelmed by the relentless suffering of another human being. How do we cope when we have to carry home a Venu's or a Thankaiyan's suffering and nurse it through the night?

Some of us are lucky to have supportive families. I often wonder how I could have coped if Chandrika and my sons were not so encouraging, or even understanding. If Chandrika had wanted a 'normal' doctor for a husband who did not transform his profession into a passion, could I have continued to travel the paths my heart led me? Often

---

[*]Government of Kerala, 'Health & Welfare Department – Formulation and declaration of State Policy for Pain & Palliative Care Services – Orders issued', 15 April 2008, available at <document.kerala.gov.in>.

she lived a lonely life for weeks when my work would tug me away to distant shores.

As a palliative care volunteer, she quietly withdraws into the background, but steps in to do what needs to be done, be it contributing part of her earnings, nagging relatives and friends for donations when the funds run low, or distributing brochures when there is no one else to do it.

But not every palliative care worker is as lucky. Time and again, I have seen people succumbing to pressure from family and choosing a conventional career. I have also seen several colleagues doggedly pursuing their chosen path and deriving satisfaction from it during the day, only to go back home in the evenings to fight their own personal battles. What sustains them? What motivates them?

Mostly, it is the intoxicating satisfaction from the enormous difference that one is able to make to human lives. It is spiritually uplifting to be able to go to bed holding the warm memory of a grateful smile on a face which had such despair a while ago. But, what about the occasions when a palliative care worker gets little support from family and, on top of that, feels like a total failure as I did in the case of Thankaiyan?

We cope by accepting the fact that we are but human and cannot always help everyone to the extent they may need. We try to recall all those lives we had been able to better, and feel a little comforted. We also share our torment with colleagues, who are ready to listen; we know we have to be there for one another. This sharing may not happen spontaneously with everyone. There is a real risk of depression or burn out, particularly with introverts. Every palliative care team must create a community within itself that encourages sharing and listening, so no one has to fight their own demons alone.

NEW BEGINNING; MORE LEARNINGS

*For there was never yet philosopher
That could endure the toothache patiently....*

—William Shakespeare[*]

---

[*]*Much About Nothing*, Act V, Scene 1, available at <http://shakespeare.mit.edu/much_ado/much_ado.5.1.html>.

TWENTY-SIX

GOING HOME

The Kerala government used to show doctors the door at the age of fifty-five. That was the mandatory age of retirement; the rule had been established half a century ago when the average life expectancy was much shorter. Well, the practice had simply continued. I retired from government service at the start of the new millennium. It was time to leave Calicut and the Pain and Palliative Care Society.

I decided to set up a palliative care centre in another city and to lay the foundation of a new endeavour to take palliative care to the national level. This was indeed an ambitious project. Kerala had only less than 3 per cent of India's population. Palliative care was available only to about 1 per cent of Indians.[*]

But leaving Calicut turned out to be more traumatic for me than I expected. I had lived in that city for sixteen years—the longest stretch I had spent anywhere in my entire life. I had spent the most meaningful period of my life here. Chandrika and I had moved to Calicut when our sons were three and four; now they were grown men,

---

[*]M. R. Rajagopal and David E. Joranson, 'India: Opioid Availability— An Update', *JPSM*, Vol. 33, Issue 5, 1 May 2007.

testing their wings to fly out into the wide world. And, most importantly, it was the place where I had nurtured my dream about treating suffering and made it real.

I had become so emotionally attached to the team that I found it hard to leave. I visited the earliest champions, Meena and Lissy, in their homes to say goodbye, somehow feeling I was deserting them.

On my last evening in Calicut, I walked across to the new Institute of Palliative Medicine building, the construction of which was now completed. I walked through its corridors in the fading sunlight. A lot of Bruce Davis, the philanthropist, was in the building; it was his dream. He had not only funded the construction costs but had also given it his heart.

It was my dream too; I had visions of it being a place of love more than anything else. I knew it was in capable hands, in more capable hands than mine, I truly believed. I felt a personal, selfish kind of grief for I would not be a part of it any more.

I found a job in a corporate hospital with a charitable intent in Kochi, which allowed me to work in anaesthesiology and palliative care. At around the same time, with the support of several like-minded friends, I established Pallium India, a registered charitable trust to promote development of palliative care throughout the country. It was financially backed by our good friend Bruce Davis, and a few others.

But I had limited time and opportunity to work for the Pallium India mission. At the peak of my frustration, a young man whom I did not know personally and whom I still have not met, sent a message through my nephew Binod: 'Tell him if he wants to do what he really wants to do, he should not be anyone's employee.'

That was like a revelation, though in a way it was a statement of the obvious. There cannot be many employers in the world who would say, 'I shall pay you; do whatever you want to do.'

I took the advice, and decided that I could easily live on my pension from the Government of Kerala, and in 2006, I left the job and moved to my birthplace, Trivandrum. This was where Chandrika and I were born; we had done our schooling and finished our basic medical education here. Our extended families lived here, and it felt like coming home. But, at the same time, I had been away from Trivandrum through much of my productive life, and I had very few friends there. I did not know people who mattered. How would I get started?

At Trivandrum, a few people joined me as volunteers, people who continue to be the quiet, hardly visible pillars of Pallium India—like my friend of many years, Dr Mohanan. I wanted to team up with my alma mater, the government medical college, to work as its non-government partner. The proposal was rejected at that time. I approached several major private hospitals, and finally, two hospitals offered me free space along with the permission to give free treatment to poor patients. This was gratifying; at least two hospital owners acknowledged the value of palliative care and trusted me.

I chose Dr Bharath Chandran's S.U.T hospital primarily because the institution already had a doctor trained in palliative care, Dr Nirmala. The good doctor had more God in her than most people. We employed three staff members—Sheeba, a nurse, Preetha, for secretarial assistance, and Nandan, who owned a car to drive us around for home visits—and a few volunteers.

Engaging the community in a new place was the next challenge. I decided to join hands with Dr Biju Soman, whose institution was at that time doing some public engagement programme, alongside elected representatives of local self-government organizations. His team was working closely with primary health centres (PHC) in a couple of places. With his permission, I would tag along with him to his monthly PHC meetings in Vizhinjam. Dr Biju set aside fifteen minutes each time for me to talk about palliative care. The first time I talked about palliative care, I failed to stir any interest. I tried again the next month. This time after my talk, a young man from my village, Sreekumar, an elected representative, got up and said, 'This is important. We must do this.'

Refusing to be discouraged by the many impassive or sceptical faces, we forged ahead. After the first volunteers' meet organized by Sreekumar, we set up a training course for volunteers, and then a weekly palliative care outpatient clinic housed in the village's public library. Next, we began doing home visits as well. Seeing our work, many people approached us to help them start similar initiatives in other areas. One of them was a group of retired school teachers in Palode. We trained their volunteers and set up a clinic inside a local primary school held every Saturday, with home visits in the afternoon.

Typically, in each of those villages or towns, the local champions would assemble a group of people together and find free space for our team to work. Pallium India would train the volunteers and the group would find the patients. But they needed guidance to get organized. We used to encourage them to register themselves as independent, non-governmental organizations to build ownership and accountability. We continued to follow a policy that we had adopted in Calicut; the individual units were not our 'branches'. Each was independent, the protagonists were responsible for their own program; they owned it. We called them 'link centres'. We believed this was essential to ensure sustainability.

In Trivandrum, I found plenty of people warning me, 'What was successful in Calicut is not going to work in Trivandrum. This place is different; people here are selfish.' I have heard this repeated in every new place we tried to involve the community. Honestly, it was not hard at all to get the community to participate in palliative care in any of the places where we opened our doors to them. How could there be any community anywhere in the world, where there are no people with compassion who are eager to help others and thus find added meaning in their own lives? They only need a catalytic force. A facilitator was essential.

So the service went on, our parent unit stepping in to provide whatever each local unit did not have, such as doctors and nurses, medicines. Gradually, some of the units achieved varying levels of independence.

We ran an outpatient clinic and an inpatient service in the parent unit, mostly for symptom control and end of life care. We started educational programmes for volunteers and professionals.

Pallium India started working with palliative care enthusiasts and interested institutions outside Kerala to initiate palliative care services. For instance, we worked with tertiary care medical institutions in many states in India to set up palliative care services or to upscale them. We trained a large number of doctors and nurses in palliative care.

Our vision was to integrate palliative care into healthcare at the national level. We were doing that by working with the central and state governments to influence policy by improving access to palliative education and by catalysing development of palliative care centres. By working with institutions and individuals, we tried to make palliative care (or at least some elements of it like pain management) part of all their healthcare practices. In each of these places, we could see the transformation of lives till then steeped in suffering. Furrows in foreheads would vanish and smiles would replace groans—it was almost magical.

TWENTY-SEVEN

A SCAR ON A NECK

I don't know which spoke to me more—the scar on his neck or the look on his face.

Ramesh was in sheer agony and, to him, doctors and the medical system were uncaring and distant. He was a young family man with a not-too-uncommon disease: a block in the blood vessels going to his leg. This condition causes one of the worst kinds of pain that a human being can have. The sufferer is unable even to describe the nature of the pain. Unlike some cancer pains, this is continuous and intense. With time, the pain keeps on growing and a person becomes all pain. They cannot think clearly any more. Concern about loved ones may give way to concern for their own pain and nothing else.

Ramesh's eyes conveyed the telling combination of hopelessness and despair. If he could think rationally, he would have told his children, 'I wish I did not have to focus on my pain so much. I love you. But please understand, I really have no choice.'

The pain had started almost a year earlier. It began in his big toe which had become blue, and he had to undergo several investigations. The imaging showed where the vessel was blocked. The doctors debated whether a bypass surgery of the vessel on his leg would help. They debated because his smaller blood vessels beyond it were also diseased and it was questionable how far the surgery would help. After several discussions at Ramesh's bedside, they decided to do an artificial bypass to connect the blood vessel to the large artery in his thigh. The bypass would start from above the site of the block and connect it below.

But there were stumbling blocks. For one thing, this would need many hours of operation time in a general surgery unit in that busy government hospital. The cardiovascular surgery department wanted no part of it. A very interesting aspect of my profession is that disease management also follows a hierarchy. Coronary bypass surgery following a heart attack is considered important. There is drama; there is glamour. It will get done. But a blood vessel in a leg? Not many hospitals give enough attention to it, especially for the poor.

The department of general surgery decided to perform the procedure. But the government did not provide the disposable bypass device needed for the operation. It would cost Rs 25,000. Would Ramesh be able to pay and be willing to go through the operation?

All his reserve funds had been drained by this time. The family went on a borrowing–begging spree. Every relative was approached. It took time, but finally they had raised the money. Several medicines were prescribed to him, all aimed at improving the blood flow, all of which, according to available evidence, had not proved to improve the blood flow enough to restore circulation in the limb. Some of the money collected went towards his daily medicine needs. Spending on food in the home, including for the children, was slashed. They ate low-cost tapioca and often nothing else.

When they had scraped together Rs 25,000, they went back to the hospital. But his surgery kept getting postponed—first, because of the annual maintenance of the operating theatres and secondly, because the backlog of more urgent patients had to be cleared.

'Come back later,' he was told.

He tried everything—talking to the local legislator for a letter of recommendation; bribing someone who claimed to be influential, which only meant that more money was lost—but nothing worked. When he went back on the appointed day, he was readmitted to the hospital. The imaging had to be repeated. Would there be enough left for the purchase of the device?

After three days, he was given the verdict: they would not operate. The surgical unit decided that the operation was not worthwhile after all. He was sent back home with a prescription for five medicines, none of which was an effective painkiller for him. The next day, as his wife was going out, he told her to take the money and repay some of the debt.

A little while later, his children playing outside the house heard some noise and ran in. Their father was hanging from the ceiling and struggling. The children, eleven and eight years old, caught hold of his legs and saved his life. Their screams brought in the neighbours who cut the rope and took him down. Ramesh was back in the emergency room of the hospital with a nasty scar around his neck.

'You had all better disappear before the doctor comes. He would report it to the police. Attempted suicide is a criminal act. There will be a police case against him, and they would question the family to probe if they were involved in the crime,' a kind staff member in the emergency room told the family in private.

Scared, the family took him out, lay him down on a concrete slab on the pavement while they debated what to do next. The inconsolable wife went on sobbing and the children looked on helplessly.

When the medical system had turned its back, two autorickshaw drivers came forward to help. Those two human beings had seen our work when they had been hired to transport patients to us. They had not studied the art and science of 'therapeutic distancing' and so their empathy made them carry the man into a rickshaw assisted by his wife, put the rest of the family in the second rickshaw, and ride to our palliative care unit.

The pain caused by lack of blood flow is not easy to treat. In Ramesh's case, it could only be partially controlled. Of course, even that reduction in pain was a huge relief for him. And he felt that people cared for him; the staff spoke to him with empathy. They seemed to understand what he was going through.

The painkiller prescribed to him earlier could damage his kidney, if he were dehydrated or if he had an overdose. Not knowing the consequences and in desperation from the pain, he had taken several tablets at a time when he was supposed to take only one. On investigating, the palliative care team found that his kidney had indeed started malfunctioning.

In hospitals, one often hears the phrase 'there is nothing more we can do' when cure is not possible. This is just not true. There is a lot we can do to care as the palliative care team demonstrated in Ramesh's instance. Pain relief could be optimized even though incomplete. The team's conversations convinced his wife and the children that the attempted suicide was not really his fault. They understood that any one present in the room might have done the same thing if they had that kind of pain. Ramesh was relieved.

As his family gathered around him, somewhere in that sea of suffering was a bit of peace. Till his death a few days later, his pain was controlled enough to let him sleep. Even though the medicines made him a little delirious a couple of times and though he was sleepy much of the time, his suffering was by no means as intense as it had been.

A week after his death, Ramesh's wife broke custom (she was in mourning and was not supposed to go out for forty-one days) to come to our palliative care unit to thank the staff.

Remarkably, she never said a word against the cruel medical system which had allowed her husband's unbearable pain to go untreated. But that kind of suffering is continuing to this day and should be on our collective conscience when we boast about the healthcare in the country.

TWENTY-EIGHT

KERALA PALLIATIVE CARE POLICY

Many slashed wrists, scarred necks, bruised minds, and wrecked lives convinced my colleagues and me that starting new palliative care units would still be an inadequate solution to the suffering of people with illnesses. Palliative care needed to be part of hospital care along with diagnostic and curative interventions. Could we persuade the Government of Kerala to adopt a palliative care policy?

A personal connection of a colleague with the chief secretary (the head of the executive) of the state opened a gate. Pallium India submitted a proposal in 2005 for creation of a state palliative care policy. This yielded results. The Department of Health created a working group to draft a policy document. Several meetings and a lot of hard work later, in 2008, Kerala became possibly the first government in a low–middle-income country to declare and operationalize a palliative care policy.

Today, every single primary health centre in Kerala has one trained nurse dedicated to palliative care work. Mostly, every bed-bound patient gets at least one visit by this nurse, at least once a month. Many things that had necessitated an onerous travel to a hospital earlier, like the need to change a urinary catheter, happen at home now. Also, this policy has critically lowered the burden of healthcare costs for the patient and the family.

However, when someone compliments Kerala on its palliative care success, I remember a news item that appeared in the *Times of India* in 2014. In a hospital in the north Kerala city of Kanhangad, a couple killed their son and then themselves. According to the police, they had left a note saying that they could no longer bear to see their son in pain.[*]

Even with all the fanfare surrounding palliative care, Kerala's provision for pain management is abysmally low. The state's per capita medical morphine consumption was 1.67 milligrams in 2014. True; this was way above the national average which was only 0.11 milligrams. But to put this all into context, in the UK, in 2014, the per capita consumption of morphine was 241 milligrams, while the global mean, though it includes many countries with no medical opioid access at all, was 6.27 milligrams.[**] Improvement since that year has been minimal.

Fortunately, there is some good news. Though much too slowly, more and more doctors are getting trained in palliative care. The Kerala University of Health Sciences, in 2016, incorporated palliative care into the existing curriculum. And thanks to a decision by the Medical Council of India (now replaced by National Medical Commission), palliative care has been included in the curriculum for medical students

---

[*] TNN, 'Parents kill ailing son before committing suicide in hospital', *Times of India*, 2 June 2014.
[**] M. R. Rajagopal, Safiya Karim, and Christopher M. Booth, 'Oral Morphine Use in South India: A Population-based Study', *Journal of Global Oncology*, Vol. 3, No. 6, December 2017, pp. 720–27.

from 2019.[*] It includes various elements of palliative care, namely pain management, end of life care as well as attitude, ethics, and communication.

A major subject missing is the management of symptoms other than pain. Pallium India has created teaching packages in the various domains of palliative care, incorporating symptoms other than pain as part of end of life care.

And in 2019, when Pallium India requested a revision of Kerala's palliative care policy, it was warmly received by the Department of Health. The new policy made clear plans for starting palliative care divisions in medical colleges so that medical students would learn palliative care. These would grow into palliative care departments in the next five years. The new policy also spelt out ways for government–NGO participation and concerted action.[**] As a new feature, it included a plan for the formation of a palliative care grid with virtual and collaborative sharing of information.

Unfortunately, the implementation of the revised palliative care policy was stalled due to the COVID-19 pandemic. The challenge will be to fill the implementation gap.

---

[*]Medical Council of India, 'Competency based undergraduate curriculum for the Indian Medical Graduate', available at <https://www.nmc.org.in/wp-content/uploads/2020/01/UG-Curriculum-Vol-III.pdf>.
[**]'Rights-based approach for palliative care', *The Hindu*, 11 December 2019.

TWENTY-NINE

PAIN MISUNDERSTOOD WORLD OVER

Sunshine was one of the good friends I made at a three-day palliative care workshop organized by Nancy Hinds in Fresno, California in 2010. Sunshine became a friend for life.

After a stint as a volunteer at a nursing home, she was eager to know more about palliative care. Fascinated by our work in India, she travelled to Trivandrum to spend three months with us. For years, Sunshine continued to help us with our advocacy work in palliative care. She also started spending more time on what she loved best—writing; telling stories.

She had just published a memoir titled *When My Boyfriend was a Girl*, which was on its way to success. She was interviewed by a major podcast, had lined up television and radio interviews, and newspapers were reviewing her book. Life was good.

Three days later, she was in an outdoor restaurant celebrating with friends, when calamity struck. While a worker was replacing the propane tank on a large heat lamp, it toppled and struck her on the back of the head, twisting her neck.

In the emergency room, the X-rays and MRI scans showed no bone injury. Initially, there was no pain, but soon she was in agony.

Hearing her story from faraway, it sounded like she had a crush injury on her neck, bruising her nerves. Nerves have the task of carrying pain messages and other sensations to the brain and the slightest irritation to a nerve can cause enormous pain—and pain has a way of self-perpetuating. Remember, pain is essentially protective. It is meant to give a warning, 'Run away from this danger. Escape!' With the best of intentions, pain tightens muscles splinting the injured part, reducing any movement. This protective reflex is great if you can run away. It's useful if the splinting action is helpful. But often it is not so.

Sunshine's particular misfortune was to sustain the injury on the neck. The neck is anatomically peculiar. An obviously important part connecting the brain to the rest of the body, it has to accommodate many vital structures—the spinal cord and great vessels taking blood to and from the brain, the breathing tube, and the food pipe—all crammed into a narrow cylindrical area.

The consequences of muscular reaction to pain, therefore, can be significant. Tight muscles straighten the neck compressing the nerves that pass between the bones, causing severe pain. You know how painful it can be when you get a cramp in a leg muscle. Imagine that kind of cramp or worse happening in the neck for days and weeks.

Gradually, the tight muscles themselves generate pain-producing chemicals magnifying the pain. And the nervous system itself becomes high-strung, every stimulus causing more and more signals to reach the brain. 'Run away, run away, escape!' the blind protective system keeps yelling. But in this situation, there is no way of running away from your own body. You can only run into a hospital seeking help.

It would have been a great blessing to Sunshine if the staff in the emergency room on that day had understood this phenomenon. We call it central sensitization or the 'wind-up' of the nervous system because it is like winding up a spring and tightening it. The sooner you treat central sensitization effectively, the more successful the treatment and the better the outcome.

But then and now, the world over, pain seems to be poorly understood and taught. Diseases are given importance; pain or suffering is ignored.

I used to have frequent e-mail communication with Sunshine's husband. All the descriptions suggested to me that it was central sensitization and it needed immediate attention. But the healthcare system available to Sunshine at that time did not seem responsive to these ideas.

Here was somebody who did not fit a convenient framework of diseases and, because of that, she was not getting proper attention. I was afraid that any wasted time might make the pain untreatable.

Possibly a bigger issue was 'opiophobia' (an unreasonable fear of opioids) following the opioid epidemic in the USA. Opioids have been used successfully to treat pain safely and effectively in the UK and many other countries for decades without significant diversion for non-medical use. But a strange pharma industry driven problem occurred in the United States. The irrational promotion of opioid analgesics is said to have resulted in diversion of opioids contributing to the addiction issue.

The inevitable reaction came; the pendulum swung back. Predictably, it did not assume a central balanced position; it swung all the way to the other extreme, as any pendulum would. New tightened guidelines appeared. Doctors started avoiding opioids. As a consequence, Sunshine was deprived of much-needed pain relief, as do many thousands, if not millions, of people in pain.

With all the advances in medical science and pain management in the US, I was sure that American pain specialists would treat her pain knowledgeably and effectively. The problem was getting Sunshine into the system.

When her husband consulted me, I felt that she needed enough pain relief to get the muscles to relax and to get the abnormal muscles and the abnormal nerves to behave normally. Several medications could assist the process. And if none worked, one could administer powerful medicines through a catheter inserted into the epidural space in her neck between two layers of the covering of the spinal cord. That could ensure adequate pain relief and reverse the central sensitization which threatened to destroy her physically and emotionally.

On my prodding, Sunshine and her husband gently suggested some such measures to a pain doctor. The response, I was told, was that it could not be done. Later, she emailed me about her experience, 'My primary care doctor (referred by a mutual physician friend) told me every single one of my symptoms came down to anxiety. She refused to give me any medications at all and didn't even make any referrals. To her, I was a head case, plain and simple. And most of the other doctors I saw were the same. They were constantly talking about behavioural therapy, as if my pain would magically disappear if I saw a psychologist. One of the doctors told me that all I needed to recover was psychotherapy. And this is what I mean about what's happened to pain medicine overall. There's a good side in that there's more recognition that people need emotional support and help coping with the pain. But it has gone way too far and at this point doctors have ceded any responsibility and treat almost all pain sufferers as head cases.'

When I finally met her in her home in California four months after her accident, I could not believe what I saw. She was just skin and bones. She had lost a quarter of her body weight and now weighed less than forty-five kilograms. She was retching continually and was unable to hold down any food. Her whole body was rigid. She was afraid of every single moment and movement.

I moved forward to take her hand; she drew back imperceptibly, a slight flinch that warned me not to touch her. No touch could be borne. She had been a cat lover, but now she had to keep the cats away. Her husband explained (Sunshine could hardly talk) that a few days earlier a cat, obviously impatient for a caress, had jumped on to her lap. This had worsened the pain to an intensity from which she had still not recovered. What I saw was a person slowly dying in suffering.

With her permission, I sent an email to every pain physician and palliative care physician I knew in the US. I explained her inability to access the medical care that she sorely needed and sought help on her behalf.

Thankfully, there were many responses. It was so reassuring to find that a lot of people cared. Latching on to a solution that was offered close by, we made an appointment with a famous pain management centre. Sunshine's insurance did not cover treatment there, but her husband thought they could somehow find the money.

I accompanied Sunshine and her husband to the clinic. The forty-five-minute drive was agony for her. Sitting in a car was tough, moving to a wheelchair was torture, and being wheeled to the clinic was hell.

The unsmiling doctor who greeted us appeared to be a resident. He took her history, did the examination and gave the verdict that she could be treated there; but she would need several consultations and a long process before they could start the treatment.

Sunshine was despondent. She pleaded, 'But my pain is ten out of ten; I cannot imagine anything worse; I cannot wait for these weeks; I need treatment now!'

He called in a senior person, who was obviously a consultant. He asked Sunshine what she thought was wrong with her. She suggested that it could be as I had explained—central sensitization. He didn't disagree. He explained that before they started any treatment, Sunshine would need a consultation with a physiotherapist and a psychiatrist. The physiotherapy consultation could happen in two weeks, but for the psychiatry consultation she would have to wait a month.

The emphasis on the psychiatry consultation was a common feature in the conversation of both doctors. There seemed to be an assumption that Sunshine's pain could be primarily a manifestation of anxiety. Neither considered the obvious—that she seemed anxious because she was in agony and her life had been thrown into chaos.

'Give me something for the pain,' Sunshine pleaded. 'I

cannot bear this pain. The travel to this place has worsened it beyond imagination.'

They refused.

'We do not write prescriptions, but we will make a recommendation. You will have to go back to your general practitioner for any prescription.'

'How can it be?' There was sadness, anger, and disbelief in Sunshine's voice. 'How can a pain management place send me away without relieving my pain?'

'I am sorry,' responded the doctor, with a forced smile on his face. 'That is the procedure.'

I tried to intervene, pointing out the possible consequence of months more of pain in a person who was throwing up constantly, not even retaining oral medications, and had lost almost twenty kilograms in four months. Didn't she require emergency treatment? The doctor did not budge.

Somehow, that same evening, Sunshine's husband tracked down a doctor she had seen previously. He prescribed an opioid medication after seeing the notes from this famous clinic we had visited. Her previous records had shown that her pain did respond to opioids at least partially. She could hope for some pain relief and a relatively peaceful weekend.

But how could she wait for months for the treatment? She was in a state of pain crisis even though the MRI was normal. Here was a cruel reality. Pain didn't seem to matter; MRI scans mattered above anything else.

I kept trying other options through many kind-hearted palliative care and pain professionals who had responded to my earlier plea. The pain management service of a hospital in the adjoining city offered to admit Sunshine as a hospital patient. She received intravenous ketamine, opioids, and other medications. In a day, her vomiting had subsided, she started taking some nourishment. Her pain was still severe; but bearable.

They saved Sunshine's life.

In a few weeks, she was back at home with partial relief and enough medicines; but with no long-term plans for continued treatment.

Eventually, she got a series of corticosteroid epidurals. She also found an empathetic person in a chiropractor. With his treatment and with continued medications prescribed by the earlier hospital, her pain gradually reduced. Over several months, her requirement of opioids came down and she weaned herself off them in a year.

I had assumed that someone in her situation in her country would have received quality care. She belonged to the middle class and had good insurance. She lived in an area with top rated doctors and hospitals. Instead, I discovered that even in the US, with all its scientific advances, people in pain can be dismissed as psychiatric 'cases' and left with few treatment options. Despite my decades of experience with people in pain, I was shocked.

Unfortunately, seven years down the road, Sunshine hasn't recovered fully, though her pain is better controlled. But because she lost that all-important window in the first few months, her neck is now permanently stiff. This has led to all kinds of secondary problems, including weakness and pain that spreads throughout her body with the slightest wrong move.

As she puts it, she's locked in a pain prison. It's a tragic story that could've been avoided if just one doctor had more awareness of the process of pain and acted quickly early in the game.

THIRTY

A LIFE LESSON

In palliative care, you come across many patients and their families grappling with chaos. They are in the midst of a crisis, going through one of the worst times in their lives. It is a confusing and frightening time, and families need to share their feelings even if they don't know how to. The onus is on the palliative care worker to sit down with them and gently convey to them that you truly care. Once you stand on that threshold, you will find that they give you the huge privilege of opening up their lives to you. They let you enter an extremely private and intimate space. You learn so much, and you learn not to judge. You come across stories that will stop you from stereotyping people.

Pathumma's story was one such eye-opener for me. Sadly, I got to know her true nature only after her death. She was, to me, just another patient in our palliative care ward suffering from advanced cancer. This was clearly my fault. As Harvey Chochinov, a Canadian academic and psychiatrist from Winnipeg, the founder of dignity therapy, says, 'Treating a patient's severe arthritis and not knowing their core identity as a musician; providing care to a woman with metastatic breast cancer and not knowing she is the sole carer for two young children;

attempting to support a dying patient and not knowing he or she is devoutly religious—each of these scenarios is equivalent to attempting to operate in the dark.'*

Pathumma chose to check into the palliative care ward because her illness was getting in the way of the day-to-day functioning of her large extended family. As it turned out, she spent the last two weeks of her life with us.

Her main caregiver was her quiet daughter-in-law, Synaba, who stayed with her in the ward. Synaba rarely spoke. Pathumma's son Rehman would drop in after work in the evenings and return home to his children. Eventually, Pathumma died.

A week later, her son Rehman wanted my help. He was apologetic because he believed that what he was asking for was beyond the scope of my work. I assured him that this was not outside the purview of my work; that palliative care was for the patient and the family, and therefore our work does not end with the patient's death. He seemed relieved, and the real story emerged.

His marriage had been an arranged one, which was not unusual. However, what was unusual was Pathumma's obstinate stand against accepting dowry. She was against it. Also, another problem had arisen before their marriage. Pathumma's family had found out that Synaba had a mental illness after she was spotted at a psychiatrist's clinic. Several elders advised cancelling the engagement. The girl's family admitted that, at the age of sixteen, Synaba had spiralled

---

*H. M. Chochinov, 'Dignity and the essence of medicine: the A, B, C, and D of dignity conserving car', *BMJ (Clinical research ed.)*, Vol. 335, No. 7612, 2007, pp. 184–87.

into depression but after treatment with anti-depressants, she had recovered. She had visited the psychiatrist to ensure that she was clinically fit to marry. The psychiatrist had in fact given her the go-ahead.

Synaba's family acknowledged that they had concealed the illness since they were worried about the reaction from the boy's family.

In the midst of this uproar, Pathumma had taken her son aside and advised him not to abandon her.

'Imagine what her life would be if you reject her. Is it not almost certain that she will slip back into depression? The chance of saving her life would be gone. Get her permission, son. Go and talk to the psychiatrist; find out the details. Think hard, son, you have no father to guide you; you must decide whatever seems right to you.'

Rehman remembered holding her hands and sobbing uncontrollably. It was not because the girl he is to marry had suffered from a psychiatric illness but because he realized that his amazing mother, who had battled the world to bring him up on her own, was showing him the right path. I wonder whether he also realized that she must have been lonely. A person who thinks differently from most ordinary human beings and yet manages to be an integral part of larger family and society has to be lonely in a crowd.

Rehman followed his mother's advice. With the permission of the girl's family, the psychiatrist gave him the details he sought and assured him she was all right. His marriage turned out to be a happy one since she was a loving wife and doted on him.

His only complaint had been that Synaba, who absolutely worshipped her mother-in-law, was closer to his mother than to him. She took her troubles to Pathumma, who was more than a mother to her. They had shared a strong and loving bond.

Now that Pathumma was gone, the entire family was shattered. They all grieved; but their grief was nothing compared to what Synaba was going through. Synaba couldn't eat or sleep. It had been a week and she had lost weight. The family was worried about her.

When a loved one dies, it is natural for the family to grieve. The wound never ever heals completely. Nevertheless, though it takes several months, most people learn to live with their grief and carry on with the business of life. But for some people, grief assumes the gravity of a disease. It becomes an unwieldy monster that accompanies them everywhere, gets in their way, and sits on top of their chest weighing them down. When such pathological grief occurs, one needs professional help. I sent Synaba and Rehman to a psychiatrist colleague, who also works in the space of palliative care and grief.

When I met Rehman again a month later, he told me that Synaba was getting back to normal life.

'I am not only her husband now,' Rehman said, smiling. 'I am also her mother.'

We parted with an understanding that if he needed my counsel, he would come back. But he never did.

Sometimes, as doctors, we tend to focus on the patient and forget the people around them. They also have stories to tell us, which can teach us life lessons, such as not to pigeonhole people. In India, we tend to paint all mothers-in-law with the same harsh brush.

It is not at all difficult for me to delve into my memory bank and find several exceptional stories, such as this unique and intense bond between a mom-in-law and her daughter-in-law. This is impossible in India, we think. But the Pathumma–Rehman–Synaba story tells us otherwise.

THIRTY-ONE

CONVERSATIONS ON SEX

In all my years in palliative care, the biggest elephant in our clinic has been matters related to sex. The issues around sexuality are right in front of us, suffocating and causing great anguish, but almost skilfully neglected in healthcare.

Despite the internet, streaming platforms, and social media, we still squirm and feel uncomfortable to talk about sex. While textbooks and training curricula of medical professionals include a mention of sexuality, it is as a custom addressed sketchily in practice.

Moreover, to be able to talk about something as intimate as sex, the care provider has to first establish a close and trusting relationship with the patient. Usually, the relationship is never deep enough in the real world, either because of paucity of time or the lack of expertise.

The removal of a breast or dysfunction of a sex organ can seriously affect feelings of sexual identity. The person may feel less than normal—'I am less of a man or less of a woman' or 'I am not attractive to my partner any more'—which can seriously damage their relationship. Those feelings make the person irritable or make them mistrust their partner. This often leads them to finding unintended meanings in every conversation with their loved ones.

Interestingly, if at all it is patients and family members who bring up the subject of sexuality, not professionals. I remember a young man and his wife in a busy outpatient palliative care clinic in Malappuram district. He had colon cancer and was now living with a colostomy. We talked about pain control and other issues. As the man left the room, his wife lingered and asked to talk to me alone.

The husband had indicated that he had wanted to continue having intimate sexual relations with her. She was scared considering that he was unwell. Will his health be adversely affected?

A little probing brought out more details. 'I want to pleasure him the way he likes it,' she said sharing details, 'Will the colostomy bag come in the way, will it be risky?'

'Will it make you uncomfortable to see it while you do it?' I asked.

She stood silent.

I suggested she could fashion a cloth into a cummerbund around his waist to reduce the aesthetic issue. She requested me to go with her and supervise the wrapping. The wife used a dupatta to carefully cover the colostomy bag.

'This makes it better,' she said with a grin. Her husband smiled back.

I said it may be a good idea to openly discuss sexuality issues between them. We talked for ten minutes. I gave them a few tips on irrigation of the colostomy on a regular basis or whenever needed so that it would become less of a physical barrier. I promised to arrange for one of our nurses to teach them how to irrigate the colostomy.

When the wife called me a couple of days later, she sounded happy and assured me that 'everything was just fine'.

Things do not always work out well. There was another case, where the husband never forgave his wife for disclosing something so intimate to me. We were on a home visit and there was only so much follow up we could do. The attempts by our team to engage the husband in conversation on that point always failed.

For a long time, I personally found it difficult to bring up sexuality issues in my conversation with families and patients. When I admitted to myself that my own embarrassment was the basic issue, I felt liberated. When I recognized that my lack of expertise in discussing the topic with my patients was denying an important opportunity for them to heal, I forced myself to learn. I am not there yet; but I am improving, I hope.

LIVES SHARED

Too often we underestimate the power of a touch, a smile, a kind word, a listening ear, an honest compliment or the smallest act of caring, all of which have the potential to turn a life around.

—Leo Buscaglia[*]

---

[*]Leo Buscaglia, *Born for Love: Reflections on Loving*, SLACK Incorporated, 1992, p. 232.

THIRTY-TWO

SUFFERING MATTERS

Abida, who suffered from a kind of painful chronic calcific pancreatitis, was one of the patients who followed me to my new place of work during my two moves from Calicut.

Often I feel if I had to choose between Abida's disease and cancer of the pancreas, I would opt for the latter. Not even death comes easily to end the suffering in chronic calcific pancreatitis. It goes on and on—stones accumulate within the pancreas, not only affecting its function but also causing great pain, which is not easy to control.

Abida came from the hilly terrains in the east of Kerala, not so well-connected to the plains. Her family was poor; two of her brothers were daily wage earners. It must have been a cruel blow for the family when she came down with this disease. On her part, she seemed to have little trust in doctors because she had seen so many and none could offer her succour. The pain was all-encompassing, sometimes making her crouch on all fours for hours and often leaving her thirsty and hungry since she wouldn't drink or eat while she was in pain, afraid that drinking or eating would worsen the pain.

The pain was bad enough, but when doctors failed to acknowledge the intensity of her suffering, she felt totally helpless, all alone in her world of pain. When two of them suggested that she should see a psychiatrist, the family also started doubting her incessant complaints of pain. She felt as if the world was conspiring to inflict suffering on her.

When she ended up in our pain and palliative care clinic at Calicut, the first thing we did was to acknowledge her suffering.

As tiny doses of injectable morphine trickled into her bloodstream, 1.5 milligrams every ten minutes, she gradually felt better. From a score of ten, the worst imaginable pain, it came down to five and then stayed there. Another dose of morphine only made her sleepy. This told us that the pain was only partially responsive to morphine. Often, this happens in pain arising from disease of the pancreas.

With the pain partially relieved, Abida curled up like a baby. An hour later, when she woke up, the pain was bearable. She smiled at the nurse. It was obvious that she felt she was among friends. She talked about how the pain had made life so terrible for her, about how no one understood her, and about the added blow of diabetes at her age. No one had yet told her that the diabetes had the same origin as her pain—her disease in the pancreas.

One of the mandatory tasks of the palliative care team was to give information about the disease not just to Abida but also to her family, if they wanted to know. Despite visiting many hospitals and doctors, her family knew practically nothing about her disease. Her parents wept, as the palliative care team told them about the incurable nature of her disease. We offered to keep Abida as pain free as possible, and also help her family.

The palliative care team realized that due to a prolonged

period of pain, Abida had developed mental health issues. The smallest things upset her and she would panic at the slightest provocation. Minor inconveniences would plunge her into inconsolable grief. The doctors explained to Abida and her family that some emotional lability or attention-seeking behaviour could be the natural consequences of her prolonged pain. Once she understood that, she accepted a trial of antidepressants.

After several discussions, Abida understood that medicines would reduce her pain but would be ineffective in relieving it completely. She was told about the coeliac plexus block, which involves the chemical destruction of a group of nerves in her abdomen. This would stop her brain from registering the pain. The effect would be temporary though, lasting three to nine months on average, sometimes longer, sometimes shorter.

By the time Abida decided to undergo the procedure, the imaging machine in the government hospital had broken down with no hope of repair in the near future. I had also moved from Calicut to Kochi. Abida and her family decided to travel to the hospital I was working in at that time to get the procedure done. Her village folk scraped together a purse to support her travel and treatment.

The procedure was expensive in the hospital and the money her village had raised was not enough. The palliative care team sent her to the assessor who had the authority to consider whether she deserved charity and could be given a discount.

The assessor was a much-feared person. Every day, he had to deal with people coming to persuade him of their state of poverty to be eligible for subsidized treatment. There was even a story going around of a man driving up in his own expensive car, parking it in the hospital lot, changing into a faded torn shirt and dhoti to present himself to the assessor. Understandably, the assessor was tough.

The assessor asked Abida's mother several questions and told her, 'You will get some discount; but be prepared to pay.' The palliative care team decided to raise the required amount between them, if there was a shortfall.

Abida underwent the procedure and it worked very well. She was pain free and was able to discontinue her pain medication. She was bubbling with joy. I tried to bring her expectations to a realistic level and pointed out that at some point in the future, the pain may return and then she should come back to me.

Abida chided me.

'Why are you so pessimistic? Believe in God.'

The hospital bill was considerable and Abida's mother took it to the assessor.

'We will give you some discount. How much can you pay?' he asked.

She took out a wad of currency notes wrapped up in an old newspaper and thrust it through the space under the partition to the assessor.

'Son,' she said, 'just leave enough for bus fare for the three of us to reach Nilambur. You can take the rest.'

The assessor gently handed back the money and said, 'It's okay. You don't have to pay.'

Some twenty-five years after I first saw her, I managed to visit Abida in her home some 400 kilometres away at Nilambur, a year before she died. Life had not been easy for her. Fortunately, the procedure that she underwent seemed not only to have given temporary relief, but to have reversed a cycle of events in her nervous system which had given her that intolerable pain. The pain was no longer a big trouble, but the long-term diabetes had taken its toll. Her kidneys had partially failed and she needed dialysis thrice a week for many years. But she managed to live with her multiple health issues for more than a quarter of a century, albeit with some suffering. Our palliative care team never asked whether pancreatitis qualified as a life-threatening disease. For us, any illness-related suffering mattered.

THIRTY-THREE

ANXIETY AND DISQUIET

Centuries have gone by since Paracelsus said, 'The most fundamental principle of medicine is love.'* But modern medicine has rejected that word. I truly believe that the essence of care is love.

Amaanath, mother of a four-year-old daughter, was just twenty-three when she developed a cancer in her ovary. She had some reprieve after an initial operation; but when the cancer grew back and chemotherapy did not work, the oncologist decided against further treatment. And she came to us in pain.

The pain in her abdomen was not hard to control, but what could relieve her suffering from anticipatory grief? She could not bear the thought of leaving her little daughter motherless.

Often, she would ask for time alone with me. And over time, a recurring theme emerged in our conversations. She felt sure that her husband would remarry after her death. How would a stepmother treat her child?

One day she latched on to the idea that if her husband married her younger sister the problem would be solved. It is not unheard of, for a fourteen-year-old to get married,

---

*From *The Great Art of Surgery*.

she would argue with me. The girl was even prettier than her. Or, they could just get engaged now and wait for a couple of years for the formal wedding? Amaanath would scheme and plot and repeatedly plead with me to take it up with the family. I suppose what she wanted me to do was to play matchmaker.

Of course, the husband would have none of these crazy plans. Amaanath's sister was so young, he said. She was more like a daughter to him than a potential wife. How could he even contemplate marrying a girl half his own age?

I noticed that he did not say that his loyalty was to Amaanath or that he could not think of marrying any other woman at that point in time.

Amaanath was feverish one day. When I visited her, I laid my hand on her forehead. She clutched it and held on to it, pressing it down on her forehead. And in a soft voice, she said, 'Your hand on my forehead is the only thing that gives me peace nowadays. Can't you stay a little longer?'

Thereafter, she wanted more of my time; just for me to sit with her, with my hand on her forehead or her arm, and listen to her. Some day, I guess, medical science will discover the pathway by which a loving hand on a fevered brow leads to the heart.

I could not find enough time to spend with her. Fair allocation of resources, particularly time, is a dilemma that we come across in palliative care. We could practise the highly discussed therapeutic distancing but will that not come in the way of giving the much-needed support to patients? How can we concentrate on caring if we are focusing on maintaining a distance? Obviously, we need to strike some kind of a balance.

The tumour Amaanath had in her ovary had spread

and caused a partial obstruction in her intestine. We could overcome this hurdle with several medications given in combination. That kind of treatment was not mentioned in the fat textbooks of medicine and surgery that I had studied. They talked only of cure. To learn about this form of treatment, you have to look up textbooks on palliative medicine. Well, I had learnt this treatment among other things from the walking textbook called Robert Twycross.

We did the needful to reduce the swelling around the tumour and manipulated her medication to push the intestinal contents beyond the partial obstruction. Somehow, Amaanath carried on, eating semi-solid food.

And then one day, she came to us in great distress. Her belly was bloated to thrice the size of what we had seen the previous week. It felt as hard as stone and she could hardly breathe. We tried the required palliative medicines. Nothing worked.

The surgeon said the only way to give her relief was a colostomy. A colostomy meant creating an opening on her abdomen through which faecal matter will empty into a bag. Many people live with that. But Amaanath's disease was at an advanced stage. Would she be able to withstand the surgery? Would the wound heal?

With Amaanath's consent, the surgery was finally done and her bloated abdomen returned to the original size.

Then we heard what had triggered this problem. The previous week, without Amaanath's knowledge, her husband had married another woman in a neighbouring village. When Amaanath heard about this, she was hysterical and had to be restrained. Shortly after, her abdomen had started bloating up.

The bloated feeling could be relieved by surgery; but what could relieve Amaanath's pain from the thought that her daughter already had a stepmother?

The only thing we could do was to comfort her and continue the conversation. We suggested that the family should get together to discuss it. Her extended family set aside their anger and talked to Amaanath's husband. He came over and assured Amaanath that he would allow the child to stay with her parents. And her sister also promised her that she would look after the little girl and that she would marry someone only if he agreed to accept the girl as their first child.

This was not much, perhaps. But it was a million times more than nothing. I remember many people who feel (and do not hesitate to communicate it) that our work is not worth the effort.

'Why waste money and efforts on someone with one foot already in the grave?' an important member of a humanitarian organization had once asked point-blank before blackballing our funding application.

It is not always easy to explain what we strongly believe in—that human life is important even after a person stops being productive in material terms. That it is the hallmark of a decadent society which measures the value of life in terms of money alone. Ask anyone who has lost a loved one in pain and suffering, and they will share how those memories have formed deep scars inside the core of their being.

I am convinced that my hand on Amaanath's forehead mattered, those hours of listening to her mattered, and the colostomy mattered. The family meetings mattered not only to Amaanath, but also to the whole family and particularly to her child. The knowledge that it mattered continues to enrich the lives of healthcare professionals who believe in treating the patient and their family, not just the disease.

THIRTY-FOUR

LETTING GO

When Vishnu limped into our consultation room with a walking stick and smiling face, no one could have guessed that the smile hid a sea of suffering. Equally pleasant, his wife Tara took a seat beside him.

He had multiple medical problems. His knees were bad; very bad. His neck and shoulder were in pain as well, worse than his knees. When the pain worsened, which it did ever so often, it would cause a hideous twitching in his shoulder. This was awkward in company; the twitching was also intensely painful.

This kind of a situation—multiple sources of pain—is serious. Having one kind of severe pain is bad enough. If the pain is long-standing, it gradually makes the nerves over-reactive, steadily worsening the pain day by day. And when there are two such pains, one keeps making the other worse.

The painkillers prescribed to Vishnu did not help much. He could not take too many anyway because he had a third problem: obstructive sleep apnoea (OSA). This is quite a common malady which results in a particularly noisy kind of snoring. You snore because your tongue falls back against the throat and chokes you. Ordinarily, you learn to live with it. (Those around you may find it harder to live with it than you.) Or, when it is really bad, you learn to change your position as you sleep and somehow manage to get enough air.

Today, life has dramatically changed for people with OSA due to a device called continuous positive airway pressure (CPAP) machine. The device comes with a mask, to be worn when you sleep, which ensures there is always some pressure against your airways, thus overcoming the obstruction.

In Vishnu's case, he could not use the CPAP device either. For the machine to be effective, the mask has to be reasonably tight on the face in a constant position. Vishnu could not maintain that constant position since his shoulder and neck pain made him toss and turn every few minutes, causing the mask to move, making it ineffective.

Life was unimaginably hard for him between the pain and sleep apnoea. As I listened to him, I was looking for possible treatment options. Then he came out with what he wanted.

'Can you help me die, doctor?' he asked.

The question came out of the blue and I was taken aback. He hastened to explain, 'I am not asking you to kill me. Just tell me how best I can die. Give me the right advice so that I can get out of this hell.'

He was saying all this well within earshot of his wife. My eyes went to her.

'It is OK, doctor, don't worry about me. Death is an open subject of discussion between us. He is suffering and he doesn't see any possibility of things getting better. He is only seeing a very scary prospect of pain and more pain in front of him. And he wants to escape before he breaks down under it,' she said in a low, but firm, voice.

I keep preaching that India is not ready to discuss

euthanasia, that it is the hallmark of a cultured society to discuss euthanasia only after it has ensured access to palliative care. But I also know that whatever palliative care we provide, there are some people for whom we are still not able to improve the quality of life to an acceptable level. Here, clearly, was one such person.

But I was not ready to give up. I explained to him that we needed to discuss various ways of improving his quality of life. Maybe, he could replace his knee joints as suggested by his orthopaedic surgeon?

I could also look at ways to relieve his neck pain, I told him. There were several muscular points where pain was causing the nerves to be hyperactive, leading to the formation of some sort of nodules, which were probably the source of pain. There were various ways by which we could try to relieve that pain like dry needling or injection of local anaesthetics into those spots.

I could not possibly help him die, I said, but I could try my best to ease his pain as much as possible. And I suggested, with some elements of his suffering gone, he might learn to live with the rest of it. Whatever we decided on, I assured him, I was not going to desert him. I would walk with him on his difficult journey as far as I could.

He agreed to come for more consultations and to reconsider the surgical option. Meanwhile, he continued to work, in spite of his pain. He was not as regular with his clinic visits as I would have liked. He would occasionally come in for an hour to talk to me.

And then, a few months later, I heard from a mutual friend that he had died. I must confess that my initial thought was that he must have died by suicide. But the truth was that he died of a heart attack. The worst was what he had to go through on his last day.

Tara told me what had happened. Vishnu had a terrible pain in his chest and was admitted to the intensive care unit in a big hospital, where he went through all the usual investigations including an angiography. The doctors diagnosed multiple blocks in the blood vessels of his heart. He needed surgery, but he was certainly not a good candidate. Meanwhile, the rhythm of his heartbeats had become grossly irregular.

It is interesting to note that our medical system cannot possibly give up before the last possible gadget has been tried. The system had shown little interest in treating his pain or breathing problems all these years. But they quickly put in a pacemaker, a device that generates tiny electrical signals so that the heart can beat regularly.

Vishnu was extremely uncomfortable. He begged to be allowed to sit up and pleaded with his wife. 'Please tell them, I only want to sit up. This is agony. They cannot understand my suffering, you can. Please help me.'

And she did plead to the doctors. 'You don't know the suffering that he has already been through. If it is time for him, please let him go.'

But her pleas fell on deaf ears.

'Just give him another twenty-four hours; perhaps he will be fine,' they said. For them, 'fine' was a heart beating regularly even though his life was already worse than death for him.

In a few hours, he died, suffering.

'Thank you for your understanding; thank you for listening,' Tara said. 'No one except your team acknowledged his suffering. Doctors had either ignored his pain or had asked him not to think about it.'

This kind of disease-focused treatment has become the order of the day. It ignores human suffering and concentrates on a beating heart, ventilated lungs, or a functional kidney even when a cure is not possible. The voices that point out the absurdity of it are too few and far between, as that of Sindhu, a freelance journalist from Mumbai, who wrote in *The Hindu* about what her dying father suffered through in an intensive care unit. Extremely uncomfortable, he had pleaded to not be 'tortured'. He wanted to go home.

Sindhu wrote, 'My eighty-four-year-old father, my best friend, was enduring raw, intrusive medical procedures against his own wish. All skin and bones, he looked defenceless and at the mercy of doctors, his arms tied up, vulnerable, and agonized.... But I couldn't infuriate the doctors in whose hands we had surrendered his body, and who had broken down his body into isolated segments only they could put back together again, if at all.'*

In our arrogance induced by medical knowledge, we professionals seldom realize the meaningless suffering we cause. Though every medical student has been taught that a doctor's duty is to 'cure sometimes, relieve often, and comfort always', the lesson is mostly taken as customary, and seldom registered by the medics as important. Our disease-focused and organ-centred medical care too often inflicts needless suffering.

Palliative care offers a viable alternative to aggressive life support measures in advanced incurable illnesses. It is just a

---

*'When pain is medicine', *The Hindu*, 9 August 2016.

matter of giving the right medicines aimed at comfort and a bit of compassion so that patients can start smiling, eating, and drinking again, and eventually die a compassionate death. But that is possible only if the medical system as a whole understands palliative care, and only if the person and the family understand it and are helped to reconcile with their anticipatory grief. When the family is able to shift their thinking from 'Don't give up, fight' to 'He/she must be suffering so much', they can choose palliative care and are able to send the person on their final journey under an umbrella of loving care.

But in India, we are nowhere near that point yet. Neither the average healthcare professional nor the public understands the possibilities of palliative care. Naturally, they think of euthanasia without realizing the power of palliative care. When a patient comes pleading, 'Kill me; I cannot bear this suffering,' the healthcare professional needs to be sensitive enough to empathize and ask, 'Tell me, what is it that bothers you the most?' The answer may point to one or more elements of suffering. Most requests for euthanasia would be withdrawn when the pain is relieved, or a lonely person realizes that someone does care. How can a civilized society think of euthanasia without first offering enough support to relieve people's pain or other suffering?

Having said that, in some rare instances like Vishnu's, palliative care may not succeed in improving the quality of life to a satisfactory level. But we can still continue to provide palliative care and make sure that the person does not feel alone and rejected. We may not be able to improve their physical reality sometimes. But what prevents us from continuing to be there for the person, providing companionship with empathy? 'Let me walk with you on your difficult journey; we will never abandon you,' should be our key message.

Even a long time after his death, I think of Vishnu often. I admire him for his ability to smile even in the hell that he lived. I admire Tara for being such an understanding companion. And I feel angry at the well-meaning, but eventually heartless medical system for inflicting that kind of suffering on him on his last day. They cared for his heart and not for him.

THIRTY-FIVE

GLOW IN THE DARK

When life throws challenges at you, do you bravely accept them? Or even smile through them all? An American psychiatrist Dr Elisabeth Kubler-Ross found that most people go through the classical sequence of denial, anger, bargaining, and depression before eventually coming to acceptance; most, not all. Some exceptional people meet adversities with equanimity. Some others get stuck at anger and depression.

In palliative care, we try to help patients shake off their despair as much as possible by focusing on achievable objectives. Every small achievement helps not only to make life meaningful for them but also to make them feel useful to others. This makes the quality of their life better in the limited time they may have left.

Simi was in her late twenties when she sought our care. Her father was long gone and a not-too-cheerful mother had brought up Simi and her younger sister. We had no idea what had turned her mother into a sour person, and we never really got an opportunity to find out.

Perhaps her mother, doubling up for a missing father, had been too caught up fulfilling her duties. According to Simi, she never recalled getting a warm hug from her mother. She had given both her children a good education.

She had arranged Simi's marriage with a man two years older.

The first few weeks after her marriage were the happiest time in Simi's life. And then came the revelation that the man had lied about having a job. He did not have one, and did not seem to want to work.

After the initial disappointment, Simi resigned herself to being the only earning member of the family. Along with a regular job, she worked as an insurance agent on the side, spending hours each day after her nine-to-five job seeking out clients and supplementing her income. And then, she became ill.

The diagnosis was cancer of the rectum. She was devastated; but then she became hopeful that her disease was possibly curable. Her belly was opened up; the surgeons found the tumour to be inoperable, and made a hole for the faecal matter to come out through the left side of her abdomen—a colostomy. She was shocked to wake up after the surgery with a colostomy. The doctors had not discussed it with her earlier. She never, ever, really reconciled to it.

Once her doctors had told her, 'There is nothing more we can do,' she had gone 'doctor shopping' and 'system hopping', from ayurveda to homeopathy, and then herbal medicine. Eventually, when the pain could not be borne any longer, she came to us with a request to make her pain free. An oncologist had told her that if she got stronger, he could consider trying more chemotherapy. She was pinning her hopes on such a possibility.

Apart from us, her only friend in the world seemed to be her sister. Her husband never came. When she informed him about her diagnosis, he walked out on her. She told us that after the diagnosis her husband had started nagging her for a divorce: 'Why don't you allow me to live my life? Why do you want to drag me also into all this? Let me go.'

Her pain was not easy to control. There was some relief, but it was always one thing after another. She would start vomiting and we would suspect a subacute obstruction of the intestines; but we would be wrong. We all knew that without getting her emotionally stable, improving her quality of life was very difficult. The sister, who had a job herself, was loving, but not a good communicator. Silently, she would do all that her sister physically needed, and her favourite line was, 'Everything is going to be all right. Don't worry.'

Her mother would stay with her every time she was admitted to our inpatient palliative care unit. She would help with the physical needs like changing the colostomy bag; but she was no help emotionally. Unable to sleep, Simi would sit up at night with a bed lamp and try to read. The mother would start scolding her and that would trigger a verbal battle from which only two sullen losers ever emerged.

One day, she came in with severe pain. It turned out that the precipitating factor was a legal notice served by her husband, asking for divorce. Now that she was more familiar with some of us, she spoke often about the unfairness of it all. It took her many weeks to come to a decision. She would fight the case. It was her choice; but the palliative care team helped her come to terms with the fact that she really could not afford to spend a lot on legal expenses. Eventually, she accepted that she had lost him. But she could not accept the man not wanting to return her the gold given as a dowry, which formed a major portion of the savings for the family. She never got over the feeling of being unfairly treated on all counts.

I tried to get her to talk to me as she struggled to make sense of her situation. Though she had accepted she had an incurable disease, she drew up a list of things she still wanted to do such as completing the sketch of a house that she wanted to build for herself, in which she would live with her mother and sister. Having achieved that and having put away enough of savings from her work, she wanted to go to see her spiritual guru, a god-man who had millions of worshippers across the world. She wanted to do social service. The fact that she was dreaming of things which might require many years to fructify did not dawn on her. Or maybe she refused to see things as they were. She must have known only too well that her time was limited but she was not ready to think about it or accept it.

During one of our conversations, she was, as usual, stalling any discussion on the reality of her situation. I tried to also get her prepared for the worst while hoping for the best.

It took some time, but soon I noticed that she was beginning to talk about acceptance. But she veered between harbouring unrealistic hope and acceptance. The hardest part for her was coming to terms with her husband abandoning her and wanting to keep the dowry. She felt helpless because she could do nothing about it. The law would be on her side, but the legal procedure in civil suits would take many years to come to a natural conclusion, and hence was no use to her.

Her mother seemed to continue to protect herself by being as emotionally detached as possible. The verbal sparring between them continued, yet the partial acceptance seemed to help Simi in her last few weeks. For quite some time, she had been afraid of sleeping. It took her time and a lot of help from us to realize that what she was actually afraid of was dying. Once she accepted that, her sleep became more peaceful. Her pain control was better. Though she would continue to be gloomy, the peaceful intervals were more.

When she died, her mother's eyes were dry. Life seemed to have made her embittered. The sister was tearful, yet seemed to be relieved that Simi's suffering had come to an end. And we felt we had played a small role in blunting the sharp edges of their angst and pain.

That is all we can do sometimes, play that small role, make at least the slightest difference, and never abandon anyone if we can help it.

THIRTY-SIX

NO ONE SHOULD DIE ALONE

'When will you come next?' seventy-two-year-old Karthichechi asked me.

Karthichechi (sister) had advanced oral cancer and was living in a hospice (mostly for the destitute) in Thiruvananthapuram run by a religious organization. Around fifty people lived there and were cared for by a single superhuman nurse, Sister Elizabeth (a nun) and two (during lucky months, three) trainee nurses. Despite the staff shortage, the work that Sister Elizabeth and her colleagues did was phenomenal. The place was always clean and residents well cared for.

Our palliative care team visited the institution once a week. Sister Elizabeth herself had some palliative care training, and if she needed more help, we would step in.

'When will you come next?' Karthichechi persisted.

One of the doctors from our team would be coming every week, I assured; she wasn't satisfied with my answer. Obviously, she was lonely and badly needed a friend. She would hug anyone who went close enough to her and if you sat down and talked to her, she would narrate her sad story.

As a single mother, Karthichechi had brought up her only daughter and got her married. Unfortunately, the son-in-law was an alcoholic. The daughter had to work hard to feed the family, while the husband reached home drunk in the evenings and demanded money from his wife. If she had none, he would beat her up. If the children tried to intervene, they too would get beaten. He didn't want Karthichechi staying with them. And so, she lived alone. And then she was diagnosed with cancer in her cheek.

By the time we met her, the cancer had advanced. It was incurable.

She was in excruciating pain. With morphine and paracetamol round the clock, the pain was brought under control. She managed to eat using the right side of her mouth. Her speech was slurred, but she was able to communicate. Whenever she could find anyone to listen, she talked.

Though Karthichechi was upset about her daughter's situation, she would incessantly complain about her. Her major grouse was that her daughter was not visiting her and was also pocketing her widow pension. Here was a woman clearly unhappy with her daughter, while acknowledging she was also in a no-win situation.

As her condition deteriorated, we decided that while morphine had its role, the most important treatment for her would be to meet her daughter occasionally. Several attempts later, we reached the daughter on the phone. When we explained the situation, she told us that she did not have money for the bus fare. We arranged for the money and sent it to her.

The daughter arrived. Karthichechi was angry at first, but soon mother and daughter hugged each other and cried for a long time. I still cherish the image of the daughter sitting by her mother with her hand caressing the old woman's forehead. The mother died with her daughter beside her.

Loneliness at the end of life is a tragedy afflicting the elderly world over. The suffering it causes cannot possibly be understood fully by anyone who has not experienced it. Gilly Burn once told me that when she visited a patient in a Calcutta slum and touched her arm, the woman started sobbing uncontrollably. 'It's been weeks since anyone touched me,' she confessed a few minutes later, when the sobs had subsided. Does our system recognize the loneliness epidemic?

Any civilized society has to take responsibility for the ills within it. A major reason behind the success of the palliative care movement that evolved in Kerala was community participation. Compassionate people accepted the responsibility of supporting the less fortunate around them. They helped people in multiple ways: acting as links between the patients and the medical system, offering weekly or more frequent visits, and sometimes arranging for financial support.

When we have the courage to face the issue and accept that health is not only absence of disease or infirmity but also physical, social, and mental well-being, we can focus on quality of life and address relevant psychosocial issues such as loneliness, stigma, and abandonment, even while treating the illness.

THIRTY-SEVEN

STRIPPED OF ALL RIGHTS

When a person falls sick, the family tends to take over key decision-making. When struggling with a serious illness, it is only the rare, strong individual who still manages to retain control of one's life. Usually, the family goes into a huddle to discuss where to seek treatment. They confer with the doctor, who automatically sees the family as the client. And perhaps, for the doctor, it is so much easier to talk to the family who are often less complaining than the patient.

I remember the Punnoses, a couple who was part of a promotional video recording on the need for palliative care.

'During my mother-in-law's cancer treatment, hardly any doctor talked "to" her. Everyone talked "about" her, to us, the son and the daughter-in-law,' Mrs Punnose had said.

I particularly recall this phrase that she used—doctors talking about a patient, not to her. I suppose, in India, that is the fallout of the extended family structure. But it is a relevant point.

In a medical environment, the ailing person pales into insignificance juxtaposed with the disease, and this sidelining makes it harder for the patient. Even if the person tries to assert himself, the family overpowers the patient, who realizes with shock that he is no longer in control. Even if part of a loving family, the patient still feels disempowered. It is worse if the patient has some long-standing difficulties with the family.

Take the case of Seena, a young woman with a progressive neurological disease, which made her more and more incapacitated with each year. Her parents were dead. She was under the care of her brother. Her young sister-in-law resented the enormous burden and would verbally abuse her.

'Why don't you die? My God, will I have to carry this burden for the rest of my life? Or, will I be forced to commit the sin of murder?' she would curse.

We were informed of her situation by an ASHA (accredited social health activist), a medically trained woman from the community who is paid a small amount as incentive by the government. Once we heard of Seena's terrible condition, we found her a nursing home. The family was not happy with our intervention and firmly refused.

'What would people think if we sent a family member to a nursing home? Of course she will be looked after in her own home,' they told us.

All our arguments failed and we were no longer welcome at the house. The home visits stopped. Occasionally, we would get some news of Seena's troubles through the ASHA. We found it hard to accept the situation. Seena was going through unimaginable suffering. There was a simple solution available, which would make life more liveable for almost everyone concerned; yet to keep up appearances she was being denied care. We explored all options including seeking legal counsel; and finally decided that our interventions could worsen her situation. Seena survived a year of misery and then died. To this day, we don't know what kind of death she died!

◆

Paruchechi was another elderly woman who was stripped of her autonomy. Recovering from a stroke, she had only partial use of one side of her body. We had given her a metal frame with which she could move around but she was not able to contribute to any physical work in the kitchen. The family cared for her. Her husband stayed at home beside her, while Paru's two daughters moved from the neighbouring town to look after her. The grandchildren had to leave their city school and move to the village school. Quite a lot of sacrifices had been made on everybody's part; the family never missed an opportunity to bring it up.

We used to visit Paru at home. One day she confided in us how miserable she felt about the sacrifices her family was making for her.

Her husband never failed to point out that he had stopped going out and stayed at home all the time to be with her. His entire attitude conveyed 'I am giving up my life for her'. Her daughter kept telling us how hard it was for her to move from the city to the village; how the family compromised the children's future by moving to the village school for the sake of the mother. No one said, 'We are glad we are able to do this for her.'

I looked at the woman, the topic of discussion, during the conversation. Her expression clearly said: 'I wish I were dead.'

When I wanted to discuss her mental well-being, her husband tried to brush us off. The unspoken message was:

'Can't you see how well we are taking care of her?' We could not change her family's attitude towards her. She was at their mercy. Sometimes, we are not able to cross the barrier.

Palliative care is not just about getting rid of pain. It is also about lending an ear to a patient and caring about their emotional well-being. Sometimes, when you really listen to them, you may pick up what is troubling them physically too.

◆

A colleague and I were once teaching at palliative care programmes in northeast India for professionals in two different hospitals. The plan was to spend the morning in one place, grab a quick lunch, and then rush to the other hospital in the afternoon. We were halfway through the programme, when a doctor requested me to see Zarina, a young woman with advanced cancer who was in depression. The family needed guidance. Could I help?

Of course, I was glad to do so; the problem was paucity of time. So, the doctor brought the young woman into the classroom. She would benefit from the consultation, and the participants of the programme would benefit from her experience.

Was the patient willing? Well, she was too weak to respond. The family was more than happy to have the consultation. So, just before the beginning of a session on communication, the patient was brought in. Her uncle carried her frail body up the steep stairs leading to the classroom and placed her on a sofa in front of the class.

As thirty eager pairs of eyes looked on, the girl lay on the sofa, hardly able to move. She was miserably thin; her cheekbones stood out prominently. There were furrows of suffering on her forehead. She was visibly in pain. The family looked on helplessly.

'What is bothering you the most, Zarina?' I asked her gently.

'Tired.' She replied in a faint voice.

'What else, Zarina?' I asked.

With a supreme effort, she raised a hand and touched her belly.

'Is it pain?' I asked. She nodded.

'Where else? Is it only your belly that is hurting?'

She raised her arm with a lot of effort and slowly pointed to her throat—she had pain there too.

Zarina had several problems. Part of her belly showed the protuberance of a large tumour; touching anywhere near it pushed her into agony. She opened her mouth with a huge effort after much persuasion. It was obvious; her mucus membrane was laden with thrush, the opportunistic fungal infection that attacks when immunity is low.

A doctor had suggested that she was suffering from depression because she was refusing food and drink. The family and the other doctors had latched on to the idea and contemplated giving her an antidepressant. But when they once attempted to put a nasogastric tube, the girl had pulled it out. The doctors and family were reluctant to try it again, fortunately for her.

The little information Zarina had given us indicated another picture. It was not depression. Here was a girl obviously in an advanced state of malnutrition, in excruciating pain, unable to speak and swallow because of her weakness and the thrush.

Zarina was admitted to a palliative care centre. With

morphine given through an intravenous cannula in titrated doses, her pain was brought under control. She got some fluids to treat her dehydration. An antifungal injection over the next few days began to get rid of her thrush. She could not eat much, yet. But, at least, she could swallow some fluids.

I was hoping to be rewarded with a smile from Zarina before I left the city. But it did not happen. She lived reasonably pain free, but her disease was too far advanced to be reversed. Her general condition deteriorated and she died in a few days.

The participants of the seminar on that day certainly learnt something about pain management and about assessment and treatment of thrush. Much more importantly, I believe, they learnt the value of sitting with a patient, talking directly, and listening actively.

THIRTY-EIGHT

IMPRISONED IN AN EMOTIONAL FORTRESS

Shaji, a lawyer by profession, reminded me of the strong, silent man I'd seen in Hollywood movies set in the Wild West. A man in his fifties, his conversation was minimal and always restricted to his sickness, and almost exclusively about his pain and its management.

Shaji had a cancer growing out of the lower end of his spine. It had been operated on twice and irradiated, but now the cancer was back with a vengeance. He had little difficulty walking or moving; but he had trouble sitting down for any length of time.

In the year and a half of our association, I never met his family, except for one meeting with his tight-lipped son during the last few days of his life. Shaji was a successful lawyer and what he wanted out of life was control over himself. He would come for his consultations with a chauffeur. He never permitted us to visit him at home even when he became very ill. The pain was excruciating and very embarrassing for him. On a zero to ten scale, he described his pain as being at a ten. Every now and then it would reach unimaginable levels, making him suddenly writhe in agony.

'I know mercy killing is illegal in India and you will not do it, but just give me some information. What will be the safest way of taking my own life? I want to do it now, when I still have the strength,' he asked me in all seriousness during the first consultation.

During the next five minutes of our matter-of-fact conversation, he agreed to change his agenda and give us one chance to relieve his pain. We did what we usually do with excruciating pain, trying an intravenous titration of the pain with morphine. He was in the outpatient clinic, and we gave him a drug to reduce the chance of vomiting and then injected a tiny dose of morphine into a vein every ten minutes. After an hour, he could sit up with some comfort. An hour and a half later, his pain had reduced to a score of one, and he was slightly sleepy. The titration was stopped there.

Shaji permitted himself a smile. We can postpone that conversation on mercy killing, he said, and walked away with a supply of morphine. He would come every two weeks, or more often if the pain worsened, for a consultation.

Generations of doctors in India are scared of morphine because they are unfamiliar with it. Their analytical minds fail to grasp that the right dose of morphine is not dependent on body weight or body surface area, but on the intensity of pain and on the opioid sensitivity of the patient's pain. Most of our patients need anywhere from 5 to 20 milligrams of morphine every four hours; an occasional patient needs larger doses. Shaji needed 100 milligrams, every four hours.

I had expected that at some point, he might open up to me and share his feelings. But he never did.

'You have gone through a lot. What was the worst part?' I asked him once.

'Breaking down in front of you. I will never allow that to happen, ever again.' He replied with an almost malevolent stare.

The only thing that he shared with me was the desire to continue practising law for at least another year, and to be able to put his financial affairs in order. I tried to explore his emotional well-being once again at a later date.

He gave me his usual mirthless smile and was blunt. 'I know which way you are headed; but, no. Treating my pain is your job.'

Well, Shaji continued to work with the 100 milligrams of immediate release morphine every four hours. At one point, the dose rose to 150 milligrams and he still continued to practise law. He stopped a few weeks before he died and, to the best of my knowledge, in control of himself as he wanted to.

It is not easy to live with the fact that only a tiny minority of Indians, and other people in the low- and middle-income world, have access to the pain relief Shaji got. My colleagues and I are dismayed that it is all due to lack of knowledge, misconceptions, irrational fears, and lack of opportunity that suffering patients do not have access to critical, adequate pain relief.

◆

Sometimes, it is also frustrating when families shy away from using morphine because they think it is risky. They have some preconceived notions about it, and ruin any prospect of the sorely needed pain relief for the patient.

Take the case of little Lakshman, an eight-year-old boy with leukaemia. His disease was incurable; his young parents were devastated. He was not responding to chemotherapy. He was prescribed morphine to deal with his pain by the oncologist, but the parents refused. They wanted to take no risks, and to them morphine seemed risky.

They wanted to continue chemotherapy; even if there was a tiny chance of improvement, they wanted to explore it. But with each passing treatment, the child was growing angrier and more morose. At one point, the oncologist refused to do anything more. Lakshman also told his parents, 'No more.' It seemed to be some kind of declaration of independence. No one was going to touch his body again.

The boy was not speaking to his parents any more, and he did not even want to see them. He would eat only if the house help took food to him. Clearly, the boy was utterly alone. The parents came to me asking me to counsel him.

Though we had not seen the boy at the pain clinic, I felt sure that the couple needed counselling much more than the boy did. They were so obviously at the end of their tether and desperate.

'This must be very difficult for you. You are obviously suffering so much. Would you like to tell me more about how you are feeling?' I asked.

'I want you to counsel my son. Please make him accept chemotherapy. It is his only chance,' pleaded the mother.

It looked as if they would bring the child only if I agreed to their request.

'If he is in pain, it is not likely that he will benefit from any counselling. By all means, bring him. Let us also try to treat his pain. When his pain is relieved, we shall be able to understand exactly how he feels,' I said.

The mother was angry now.

'We know exactly how he feels. He is *our* son. He has given up. I don't want him to give up. I want him to fight. But we don't want him to have morphine. We don't want to take any risk. Please counsel him and make him accept chemotherapy.'

I had failed completely to convince them and they left in a huff. But the story was not so unfamiliar. Most of us who have never lost a child cannot imagine how heartbreaking it is. Who was it that said, 'You have not known grief till you have stood at the funeral of your own child?'

There is something divine but also something selfish about this kind of love, where parents are unable to see their child's suffering and keep on pushing hopeless medicines into his/her system. Time and again, I have seen anger in such children.

Paradoxically, children seem to accept incurability or death much more easily than adults. They are sad, but they adapt, if given a chance.

LOVE, CONNECTIONS, DIGNITY

*Leave this chanting and singing and telling of beads!
Whom dost thou worship in this lonely dark corner of
a temple with doors all shut?
Open thine eyes and see thy God is not before thee!
He is there where the tiller is tilling the hard ground
and where the path-maker is breaking stones.*

—Rabindranath Tagore[*]

---

[*]Verse 11, *Gitanjali*, available at <www.tagoreweb.in/Verses/gitanjali-190/leave-this-chanting-2826>.

THIRTY-NINE

CONNECTIONS

I was thirty-four years old when I figured out that I was angry with my father. This realization dawned on me when I became a father. As I marvelled at my capacity for so much love for my child, a creeping resentment also began to take hold, along with a question that grew clearer and louder in my head: 'How could my father bear to send me away to live with my grandparents at the tender age of three? How could he *reject* me in such an obvious way?'

I was careful, nevertheless, not to let on just how bitter I felt. It's likely that I tried to mask my own less than benevolent feelings by playing the dutiful son. I was meticulous in my care when it came to his health and medical concerns. But the background score in my head, faint perhaps, but persistent, was, 'Why did you send me away? Did you not need me, your own child?'

The facade finally crumpled when he took me by surprise. He was around eighty-five. I had gone over to see him one weekend, and he hugged me tight, for the first time in my life. Instinctively, every muscle in my body became tense and rigid. My arms did not go around him (something I deeply regret now). Somewhere deep in me, I was screaming in anger, 'Where were you when

I needed you?' He must have felt my lack of response. That was the first and last hug between us.

Many years later, on the fifth day following his death, when the ashes are traditionally immersed in the river, the priest made us, his children, chant a prayer. It was a prayer that sought forgiveness of the departed, for any wrong done to him by any of us. As the prayer left my lips, a strange sense of peace descended on me. In that moment, I realized how much guilt I had been living with all those years. The peace did not last, though. It was a far more fragile creature than the beast, guilt, which quickly returned to reclaim its old haunt. But, in that fleeting moment, I had seen through the crack in my armour.

I wish I had the courage to ask him the question that I was holding within and torturing myself with: why? I now realize that I did an injustice to him and to myself by not giving him a chance to explain. He probably had a good practical reason for what I saw as my exile. He too could have been nursing a regret; perhaps burdened by the guilt, he couldn't patch the disconnect between us, cross the mental barrier I had created around me. Maybe, I was so distant that he couldn't reach me emotionally.

The lack of bonding between us could have been the natural outcome of that early separation and I had nursed it with my silence. His explanation could have bridged the gap between us, and perhaps we could have ended up hugging each other physically and emotionally.

At worst, he may have reacted with anger, or perhaps it may have worsened our already strained relationship, but at least there would be some solace in having spoken the words out loud, rather than forever inhabiting this no man's land of not knowing. What I really did was to judge him without a trial and thus to punish both him and myself.

This personal experience propelled me to encourage reconciliation in the families I saw in my palliative care practice. I learnt to sit beside a person and ask, 'Tell me the story of your life.' As they talk, the farmer, the single parent, the retired government servant, or the uneducated and impoverished villager reveal the incredible tapestry of their lives, each a storehouse of experiences.

Stories reveal values, which in turn illustrate what holds meaning. It is another lesson to receive the story without judgement, with generosity. Oftentimes, many share the same nebulous question inside, 'What was the meaning of my life?'

Even when 'loving' people around them seem to do their 'duty', they are left asking themselves, 'Why am I alive?' From there to 'I wish I were dead' is just a hop.

When I am faced with this 'meaning of life' question, I remember many people who shared their stories with me, like Gopalan. He had advanced cancer in his stomach. Palliative surgery and pain medications had made life reasonably comfortable for him for a few weeks. As his food intake gradually reduced and he could not retain food inside him any longer, he came to us. We treated him with suitable medications to enable him to consume at least semi-liquids.

According to his wife, Gopalan had no vices and had taken good care of his family. His only fault in her eyes was that he had been too honest and devoted to his work. He had been the caretaker of a rich man's large estate—mostly rubber, but also coconut trees and plantain. He would start his work at the crack of dawn, hire the minimum possible labour, and do much of the work himself. He would carry his lunch with him or his wife would take it across to wherever he was. At the end of the day, he would return home to spend a little time with the family. As the children started with their homework, he would take a round of the estate on foot, a torch in his hand. His wife used to worry about his nocturnal trips: what if he came across a poisonous snake? Gopalan would wave his torch as if to say that was his protection.

Now, confined to his bed, he had to listen to his wife's rants, 'So, what did you achieve with all your commitment and honesty? You made a lot of profit for the estate owner. What did "you" get?'

When they heard he had cancer and was in hospital, the estate owner and his wife visited him and gave him five hundred rupees (a paltry sum, even by Kerala standards; perhaps a small fraction of what Gopalan had made for the owner in one day) and left. Gopalan never heard from them again. Was it not foolish to waste all his life serving someone like that, a little too sincerely?

I could see the distress and confusion on Gopalan's face. Later, I managed to get him alone, sat beside him, and encouraged him to talk.

Gopalan told me his story. He had had a hard life. Orphaned at an early age, he was brought up by an uncle and his unkind wife. He had wanted to study, but was not allowed to, and had to start doing manual work as a boy to earn his keep. He broke away from his uncle when he was old enough, worked hard to buy a small strip of land and practically built his home brick by brick. He talked about his marriage to a 'good person' though she did not always understand him. His life revolved around his wife and their two children. He was now glad that he had given the children an education and that they could live a better life than his.

He also talked about his philosophy of life, in which honesty and hard work mattered more than anything else. He believed that a healthy person had no business to be idle; a thinking person had no business to be dishonest. He believed in being completely loyal to his employer and this was what mattered most to him. But, as death waited by his bedside, he was disappointed that his wife was not appreciative of the life that he had lived. The meaning of his life was being challenged, I could see.

In all honesty, I assured him that I admired and respected him for his integrity and commitment. He was visibly relieved, I believe because I had acknowledged the qualities of honesty and sincerity that he had held precious.

Our social worker got his wife also to share her story. She had her own views about the life lived by her husband. Couldn't he have been a bit more like everybody else, caring more for himself and his family than for his employer? After listening to her, the social worker said that he understood the wife's point of view; nevertheless, we all admired Gopalan for his integrity. She was silent for quite a long time, brooding; but the social worker recognized the power of silence. Eventually she looked up with moist eyes and said, 'He is a good man'.

Later, we got the family together. We told the children how we felt, that they had reason to be proud of a father who held such noble values. His children cried when they heard this.

Gopalan also cried, but seemed to brighten up a bit after that conversation. What we had done was to acknowledge and appreciate the value he had placed on hard work and honesty. We also made his family aware of how we admired him as a person. His life did not seem so futile or meaningless to him any more. I like to believe that we gave him some spiritual solace in his last days.

What does 'spiritual care' mean to you? Does your mind immediately conjure up candles and incense? Or is it rituals, chants, and communion with God? Is it always something metaphysical, transcendent, and beyond mundane mortal realms? Or also acknowledging to someone like Gopalan that his life has not been in vain, that it was a life well worth living?

I believe spiritual well-being has its foundations in connections. I remember how much I felt drawn to my grandfather's deathbed when he was slowly withering away. And I cherish memories of my grandmother's last days for the time I spent with her. It was a painful time for her, no doubt, but I live with the satisfaction that I could be with her in those days, still connected, but accepting closure, valuing every touch and every exchange of love.

I had lived disconnected from my father, and he from me, because I did not have the courage to initiate an open discussion. This personal experience motivated me to look for broken relationships between family members. Even an imperfect repair would have been a better foundation for peace and spiritual well-being than the cracked connection we lived with. If I had listened to him and heard his side of the story, maybe we could have had an opportunity to heal.

Whenever I come across indifference, grievance, or anger in times of illness and suffering, I allow people to vent their emotions. I would refrain from giving meaningless advice like 'You should forgive him' or 'You should not speak ill of the dead'. Instead, I would acknowledge ill feelings, allow it all to come out and help the person find solutions within. I would encourage open discussions.

FORTY

WHAT MAKES GOD HAPPY?

After my mother's death, my father had chosen to live by himself with the support of live-in domestic help. He would potter around the homestead, obviously communing with (and sometimes moaning over the state of) the trees and plants that he had once tended to. One day, as he was walking around, he slipped and fell and was unable to lift himself up. Sometime later, his trusted servant found him and led him back to the house. Later, when he talked about the incident, he was unfazed.

'How does it matter?' he said. 'I just enjoyed lying under the tamarind tree.'

We, his children, flocked to his bedside. But none of us could leave our jobs to stay with him; we decided that he must move in with one of us. Succumbing to the pressure, he said he would give it a try. He chose to go with me, mainly, I think, because he was fond of Chandrika. It took us a twelve-hour drive to get to Calicut, where I lived. That evening in the unfamiliar environment, he saw his brother who had been dead for over forty years. He was confused when forced to remember the brother's cremation. He asked for an early dinner and, obviously troubled, went to bed.

'Take me back home tomorrow,' he said as he lay down. He died in his sleep within the hour.

I wish I had not imposed needless delirium and confusion on him by taking him away from his world. I wish we had allowed him to live his own life to his last day. Our intentions were good, but you know what they say—the road to hell is paved with good intentions.

It is not always possible to keep people connected to their own worlds; but we should certainly try.

Today, we often see a certain pattern. Elderly people are left alone in their homes as their children go out into a globalized world to build their lives. The children feel guilty and persuade their elders to join them in their busy world. In effect, a move away from the familiar bed and landscape outside the window becomes tantamount to exile to a strange world. You break the familiar environment, and the person is fractured.

My father got away easy; his hallucinations were not frightening. Time and again I come across horror stories— an uprooted elderly woman living in terror because she is convinced that her son is hiding a knife somewhere on his person to stab her, or a man who 'knows' that his wife has converted his home into a brothel and is terrified that his teenage daughter would be back from college the next day.

Such disconnection is at its worst when an elderly person is transferred to an intensive care unit. Delirium, which can progress to agitation, happens in up to two thirds of the elderly spending more than a day in an intensive care unit. Then, they get tied up so they do not pull the tubes and wires out. Nothing could be worse. Physical restraint increases the chance of delirium by as much as forty-four times.*

For some people, the environment assumes second place; their main connection with the universe is through God. Confronted with a fatal disease, the bonding with God often gets stronger.

Unfortunately, sometimes the reverse seems to happen. One of my patients, a man in his fifties, had retired early to spend time with his family. He had even renovated the house and was just settling in when he found that he had incurable cancer. He could not come to terms with the 'unfairness' of it all. 'Is there really a God?' he asked. 'I never harmed anyone in my life. I lived an honest life. Why would God do this to me?' When the pillar of faith is shaken, people find nothing else to lean on.

One's spiritual make up also depends on a personal belief system. I remember another elderly man in intense pain with maggots crawling around a cancerous hole in his cheek. Once he received pain relief and once we got rid of the maggots and foul smell, he willingly shared his concerns.

'What is it that bothers you the most?' I asked.

'I have prayed five times a day all my life. Now, I am not able to,' he said, eyes downcast, profound sadness writ on his face.

I hurriedly assured him that he was likely to get his strength back now that his pain had subsided. 'You will get some of your appetite back and feel strong enough to kneel and pray again,' I told him.

---

*Satomi Mori, J. R. T. Takeda, F. A. A. Carrara, et al., 'Incidence and factors related to delirium in an intensive care unit', *SciELO Brazil*, July–August 2016.

He shook his head in disagreement. 'As long as I have this ulcer on my cheek, I cannot. One needs to be clean before one prays; this ulcer keeps me unclean and I cannot pray.'

I could only hold his hand and stay with him while he grappled with his disappointment. Perhaps some skilled religious counselling could help patients tide over such spiritual suffering. But, that help must come from a religious authority, someone who is also conscious of the nature of suffering in crushing, life-limiting diseases. In the West, trained chaplains perform this role. That kind of support is not usually available in most of the low- and middle-income countries. Well-intentioned but misguided religious counselling can sometimes cause more harm by reinforcing guilt. With all good intentions, if the counsellor reaffirms what the patient fears and says, 'That's true, you cannot pray because you are unclean,' it can only worsen the suffering.

Usha Jesudasan, who lost her forty-year-old doctor–husband after prolonged incurable illness and pain, writes about dealing with the anger, loneliness, and pain before coming to terms with his impending death. She and her husband were both missionaries. She writes in her book, *I Will Lie Down in Peace*, 'Friends and relatives would visit and ask us to pray. When my children and I explain that we are praying all the time, they look at us in disbelief, as if they wanted to say, "If you were praying hard enough, he should be feeling better."'[*]

It is time palliative care training is offered to religious leaders so that they can understand the needs of people in suffering and offer the right kind of religious counsel for

---

[*]Usha Jesudasan, *I Will Lie Down in Peace*, Partridge Publishing, 2016.

the patients. For now, any compassionate human being can help enormously by just being there, listening and quietly conveying the message, 'I care for you'. Rather than preaching, this helps the person feel the presence of God. At the end of an hour or so, the person in bed might well say, 'I thought God had deserted me; He has not; He sent you to me.'

FORTY-ONE

FAITH AND RELIGION

On the subject of faith and religion, I wonder sometimes whether deeply religious people really undergo less pain or other disease-related suffering.

I remember visiting my friend and colleague of seventeen years, Dr Molly John. She had been living with cancer for many years and it had clearly advanced. Towards the end, she found herself quite breathless. Morphine controlled her pain and also her breathlessness to some extent. During my last visit to her about a week before she died, we talked about her physical discomforts first and then, I asked her, 'Molly, how do you find yourself emotionally?'

'Absolutely no problem,' she said. 'I had suffered at first. But some time back, I handed everything over to God. I am at peace.'

I suppose one does not have to be a sage to derive strength from faith. I see it all around me in my palliative care practice. But can faith also help someone to cope if the person is in constant excruciating pain?

Perhaps, it can. But I am not sure. I have read about Ramana Maharshi, the Indian sage who died in 1950. It is said that he had refused anaesthesia before an operation.

'Don't you have pain?' the surgeon asked him during the surgery.

'My body has pain, but how does it matter to me?' was his response.

Such dissociation of mind from the body has been attempted as a means of achieving pain relief since the Middle Ages. So, I have always wondered whether the mental power of these spiritual people could enable them to reach a state where they feel physical pain but do not suffer.

Maybe such dissociation is possible; but I have never seen it happen even once in the face of prolonged, agonizing pain. We are told, when Ramana Maharshi had the third recurrence of a sarcoma of the upper limb, he was heard groaning and crying out in pain at night in his last days.[*]

In the course of my palliative care practice, there were occasions I had to treat religious leaders from Hinduism, Christianity, and Islam. I am yet to see one who has conquered pain. They, however, differed from ordinary mortals in one aspect—at first, they all seemed to be reluctant to admit that they were suffering. It was as if they wanted to put up a front; as if they had no right to suffer.

I remember treating a person who lived in a monastery. Let us call her 'Nun'. Initially, she had refused to share her feelings with me. Our interactions were very matter of fact—she would describe her symptoms, accept my medicines, and call me about the reports, all very impersonal. But then, during one visit, the sadness on her face made me change the course of the conversation.

---

[*]Ruzbeh Bharucha, 'The Maharishi Ramana', *Speaking Tree*, 30 December 2014.

'Is something worrying you? Do you want to share any thoughts?'

She hesitated for several seconds before speaking. Her anxieties, as it turned out, were certainly not deeply metaphysical or spiritual; they were extremely mundane. She would like to see her biological sister once more, but both of them were in different monasteries and there were rules to overcome to meet her.

On another day, she talked about being misunderstood. Her superior was upset with her for complaining of pain and asking for a doctor. The superior felt that faith should be enough to heal her. In a burst of anger, Nun told me that she wished her superior could experience her pain, even for just a while.

Morphine could relieve her pain; but I still have the feeling that venting her emotions did her even more good. I believe I had helped lessen her spiritual pain by being a friend before whom she could shed the pretentious veneer of superhuman strength and be vulnerable and human, even for a while.

Just as I have seen faith giving strength to people, I have also frequently been a witness to the suffering and pain caused by strict religious values. Once I treated a gentleman who was breathless with advanced cancer. Morphine had reduced his pain and breathlessness up to a point, but towards the end the suffering was unbearable.

We thought he should have heavier medication which might make him sleepy but would relieve the severity of the suffering. The man agreed, but the family did not. That would be against their faith; one had to be awake when meeting the Maker after death.

'Could the family get a second opinion?' we requested.

The loving family concurred. I got them to connect me to their religious leader on the phone. He was rather dismissive, and categorically vetoed any sedation. It was not permissible, he said. Later, when the man's sons met him and explained the circumstances, he agreed. The sons were pleased; we were pleased too; but only briefly.

The gentleman's wife decided that they should not take a risk. No sedation for him.

If the issue is discussed academically in a classroom, the answer would be obvious. The man had all rights to choose his treatment. He was in full possession of his faculties and our duty was primarily to him.

That is, however, only in theory; in practice, the patient is usually too weak to fight a battle and to demand his rights against the family's wishes. And, in the real world, we cannot serve a man against his family's wish. They are the ones who bring the patient to us; if we do not do the right thing (or what they think is right), they may simply take the person away to some other doctor who would be 'kind enough'.

We have to tread carefully when it comes to religious sentiments. In Kerala, approximately 55 per cent of the population follows Hinduism, 27 per cent follows Islam, and 18 per cent Christianity.[*] Ordinarily, all live amicably together; but any perceived disrespect of religious practices could give rise to unpleasant situations.

We could have, I suppose, referred the matter to an ethics committee and wait for it give its opinion. But, this takes

---

[*] 'Kerala Population 2021 Census, Sex Ratio, Density, Literacy', available at <https://censusofindia2021.com/kerala-population-2021-census-data/>.

time, which we do not often have. In practice, we just keep working with the family, listening to them, talking to them and eventually helping them take the right decision.

But the gentleman did not wait. He died, suffering. And we palliative care practitioners live with our guilt and helplessness.

Often religion offers great spiritual beauty, but sometimes in the wrong hands, it can lead to ugly situations. I have seen a divided extended family fighting over the funeral rituals of a dead man, causing enormous grief to the wife and children.

I have not studied any religion in depth but I know enough to recognize its value in offering succour to the suffering as well as its potential to harm in the wrong hands. You can delve into the scriptures to find heights of spiritual beauty and compassion. But if you look hard enough, you can also find things that can be manipulated to spread hate.

I have found the principle of 'tat twam asi' (You and 'it' are the same) immensely comforting, telling me to look into myself or others to find God. Why do we humans find it so hard? We ignore the daily miracles happening all around us; especially in palliative care, we see miracles on a daily basis. Someone who had been writhing in pain slowly manages to sit up and regain dignity with palliative care from the team. Our volunteers from the community, with appropriate interventions from the healthcare system, give sight to the blind or make the paralysed walk. I find God in these people, in their actions, and in their love. I have never felt the need to visit places of worship to seek peace or God.

FORTY-TWO

CARE IS NOT A ONE-WAY STREET

Palliative care is supposed to be about improving the quality of life of patients and their families. Even in that definition, there is a presupposition of providers and beneficiaries—that we give, they receive. The truth is, in a spiritual sense, we often receive more than we give.

Though it is a good rule for health professionals not to have favourites among patients, I must admit that it was hard not to give a special place to Rahmath in our hearts. Few people would have lived with so many adversities in life like her. She came from a poor family, and she had an incurable, unrelenting autoimmune disease called systemic sclerosis (not to be confused with multiple sclerosis; this condition used to be called scleroderma), which gave her unbearable pain in all four limbs and elsewhere. She had already lost parts of several toes and fingers; each of those little bits of flesh and bone had meant months of unbearable pain. But she had lived through it all.

Systemic sclerosis is rare. It does not provide the opportunity for high-tech treatment and few have interest in it. Moreover, it is incurable. Certainly, it is not one of those glamorous diseases. It is a cruel disease where the body, by some quirk of fate, starts fighting itself.

Collagen, a protein that ordinarily holds the body together, is deposited all over—under the skin, on the walls of blood vessels, everywhere. And as the malady marches forward, the skin becomes tough and tight. The walls of the blood vessels thicken so much that their lumen gets narrower and blood flow diminishes. The tips of limbs are usually the first to be affected; excruciating pain is an inevitable accompaniment. Slowly, those parts turn purple and then blue. The same process can affect the blood flow to the heart and to the kidney, challenging their normal function.

With the saddest smile, Rahmath told us that her physician had given her three months to live. The kind doctor had referred her to us to relieve the pain in one finger, which was now a dirty purple and was threatening to turn blue. Every possible painkiller had been used on her except morphine. We did try morphine; it helped, but just a little.

In a fairly simple but rather dangerous procedure called stellate ganglion block, we put a needle in her neck and temporarily paralysed the nerve that tends to keep the blood vessels constricted. In a few minutes, the purple had changed to a healthier hue. The effect would only last for hours; but that might be enough to save her finger. But the procedure was risky because the blood vessel taking blood to the brain lay dangerously close. If due to some neck movement even a tiny part of the tip of the needle entered that blood vessel, even a minuscule amount of the medicine would overload the brain. The results would be seizures and possibly cardiac arrest. Rahmath found the possibility threatening, but there was no choice; she accepted the risk. So did we.

We started doing the procedure every other day. But for Rahmath, it was just not enough. The problem started in the toe, first in one foot and then in the other. The disease was relentless. For the lower limb, we needed a more complicated, but less dangerous procedure called lumbar sympathetic neurolysis.

Amazingly, she smiled through it all.

She shared her story with us—she had lost her husband when she was thirty-five years old. Since then, she had to battle many challenges on her own to bring up her children. Her life had been full of misfortune. She had little to give, yet gave plenty to the people around her in smiles, expressions of gratitude, and, always, prayers.

When I moved to my hometown, Trivandrum, to set up the Trivandrum Institute of Palliative Sciences, Rahmath decided to travel six hours each way by train to be treated by me.

She had another problem now. The nasty material deposited around her nerves started giving her excruciating pain on one side of the chest. In an ugly joke that the nerves play on themselves, she developed allodynia, touch being perceived as pain. The problem was so bad that she had to wear a loose blouse, and even had to ensure the blouse did not touch her skin.

However ill she was, she would travel back the same evening. But, without fail, she would call us the next day to thank each one of the members in the team. And she would pray for every one of us: 'That is the only thing I can do for you.'

She taught us fortitude. She smiled through suffering that few humans could cope with.

Our visiting volunteer from the US, Sunshine Mugrabi, wrote about her: 'Her smile is as wide as her face, accompanied by a bright twinkle in her bright blue-gray eyes.... When she smiles, it looks as if her entire being is infused by some wellspring of private joy. Pain cannot touch it, and in this, she touches everyone around her."*

During the last few days of her life, her suffering became intense. The palliative care team at Aluva, close to her home, took good care of her. But in the final days of her life, she insisted on coming back to us in Trivandrum. She travelled those 225 kilometres in an ambulance. She arrived at midnight breathless, blue in all four limbs and with a pain score of ten out of ten. I drove across to the hospital to meet her. Struggling for breath, she asked, could I save her?

Sitting beside her, making sure not to cause any pain with my touch, I held her arm and told her that I really did not know how long she had, but my colleagues and I would try our best to make her comfortable. Her eyes filled up with tears as she held on to my hand.

I felt so privileged that we could give her some pain relief and peace during those last few hours. Rahmath died early the next morning.

Her story does not end there. A few months later, her daughter Sunitha informed us that she was going to donate half of her very modest inheritance from her mother to Pallium India. Clearly, she had inherited all her mother's essential goodness. Sunitha struggles to eke out a living from a low-paid job. We also knew that her husband was unemployed and she had to fend for her three children. How could she afford to give money away to charity?

---

*'Letter from Trivandrum', Pallium India, 2011, available at <https://palliumindia.org/2011/03/letter-from-trivandrum>.

When we protested, she said, 'I have no choice; this is what my mother would have wanted.'

She once won a modest sum of ₹5,000 in a raffle and gave a large share of it to Pallium India. The money reached us on the tenth anniversary of Pallium India. It was an exceptional gift, worth millions.

Sunitha and Rahmath gave us spiritual care. They taught us a lot, as the people whom we treat and their families often do.

FORTY-THREE

PALLIATIVE CARE IS FOR ALL ILLNESS-RELATED SUFFERING

Most pain remains untreated in the low- and middle-income world with more than 80 per cent of the global population.[*] I believe palliative care teams in these countries cannot justify rejecting people in pain, be it acute (quick onset, short term) or chronic (slow onset, long term).

My colleagues and I have never stuck to traditional, restrictive definitions of palliative care. Instead, we have consistently done our best to take care of any person in significant suffering, be it physical pain or breathlessness; grief, anxiety, guilt, or depression; social issues, whether financial hardships, or relationship and sexuality-related matters and or even spiritual pain.

Globally, the concept of palliative care has grown too. When Dame Cicely Saunders started the compassionate revolution of palliative care, she started by caring for people dying with cancer. The concept later evolved to apply to any enduring, life-threatening disease and has been accepted to be applied from the time of the onset

---

[*]Knaul, Farmer, Krakeur, et al., 'Alleviating the access abyss in palliative care and pain relief'.

of suffering whether or not the disease is curable. Today, it is more widely accepted that palliative care should be available to anyone with serious health-related suffering, including to victims of natural disasters like earthquakes, as recommended in 2017 by the Lancet Commission on Global Access to Palliative Care. If I were to have a heart attack some day, I hope my doctor and nurse would apply the principles of palliative care while treating me. And if they are unable to help enough with my pain or anxiety, I hope the palliative care team would stand by to help.

Hopefully, a day will come when the world health assembly resolution of 2014 to integrate palliative care into all healthcare scenarios will be put into practice. Then, every doctor, every nurse, every social worker, and every other healthcare provider will incorporate palliative care into their daily practice. And then, let us hope no one who needs it will be left behind. Today, even the most modern definitions of palliative care tend to leave out a lot of suffering people, particularly in low- and middle-income countries. Someone living with paraplegia may not be counted as having serious health-related suffering in high-income countries; in poorer countries, their condition may not even be considered a suffering.

From the beginning in Calicut, our palliative care service had decided to treat people with non-cancer illness. We took on patients with chronic pain too, despite the reservations of some colleagues. Compared to cancer, chronic non-cancer pain is an altogether different kettle of fish. It often involves pain of poorly understood origin and it cannot be treated easily and sometimes can give rise to behavioural disturbances. While the average patient receiving palliative care tends to shower gratitude on doctors and nurses, some people with chronic pain who have to live with it for a lifetime of neglect by the medical profession may have little trust in any new healthcare team.

Our volunteers and staff knew then that it was not the patient's fault. Nevertheless, there were often arguments within the team in the early years about whether we shouldn't be concentrating on cancer. The usual argument against taking on non-cancer problems is that it dilutes the care for people with cancer. This argument presupposes that people with other diseases deserve palliative care less. While no palliative care team would think of discrimination in the name of age, sex, caste, or religion, here is a curious kind of discrimination, one in the name of a diagnosis. Despite the frequent questions that arose within the team which sometimes led to heated arguments, we continued to have a policy that we would not discriminate between diseases.

However, the fact remained that people with cancer were mostly referred to us. Palliative care was generally unknown, but much more unknown in the context of non-cancer diseases. Hence, it was only occasionally that people with non-cancer problems were sent to us in the early days. Sometimes, this caused a smidgen of envy.

One of our home visit teams had the experience of treating a man with advanced cancer, whose family was in dire circumstances. One of his daughters was now unable to go out and work because she had to take care of her father. She knew tailoring and on the team's recommendation, our rehabilitation service provided the girl with a sewing machine.

As the sewing machine was being carried in, the next-door neighbour wheezing on the porch gasped, 'Lucky guy! He got cancer.'

Here was the most scathing criticism of discrimination in favour of cancer patients that I had ever heard. The wheezing complainant had a long-standing lung problem (chronic obstructive lung disease) and could hardly walk a few steps. Hospitals did not like him; doctors generally prefer to see good results. Grumbling people coming back every day with breathlessness is depressing. Patients sense it by the look on our faces, which conveys the message, 'God, here he comes again!' If anything, people like that deserve palliative care all the more because in addition to all the other suffering, they are facing rejection too.

More than in creation of specialized disease-specific palliative care services, the answer lies in all healthcare providers learning the principles of person-centred care and treating suffering just as they diagnose and treat diseases.

FORTY-FOUR

ENGAGE, OR ASSIST THE HARM

Imagine a researcher, a few centuries from now, going through the history of 'modern medicine'. What would her verdict be on healthcare in the early twenty-first century?

What would she feel about the healthcare system in which, despite all the accumulated medical knowledge, more than 80 per cent of the world continues not to have access to basic pain relief?[*] Would she not ask herself: how could they be so senseless to invest so much time, energy, and money in research on 'conquering' diseases but not focus on channelling that knowledge so as to provide relief to those suffering?

What would her verdict be on our system of medical education in most parts of the world, which ignores human suffering completely and does not even teach the principles of pain and symptom control to medical and nursing students? Or, about the inexpensive opium, from which morphine is derived and which India produces out of poppy legally grown in the country, and which is

---

[*] Knaul, Farmer, Krakeur, et al., 'Alleviating the access abyss in palliative care and pain relief'.

denied to 96 per cent of Indians in pain?* About the WHO's three-step analgesic ladder, which transformed the face of pain medicine all over the high-income world, but more than three decades after its introduction, fails to reach much of the globe! Won't she call it the 'dark era of medicine'?

Even if she finds it possible to forgive that error of omission, with what phrase is she likely to describe the error of commission of our healthcare system that destroys entire families with the economic and psychosocial impact of treatment? And which she would eventually see rejecting patients when they need help most with the cruel words, 'There is nothing more we can do.' Or how in the last few days of their lives, when they need a human touch, companionship of loved ones, and rational measures for the management of pain, breathlessness, delirium, or other symptoms, they are condemned to rigorous solitary imprisonment in air-conditioned intensive care units (ICU). What would her verdict be about that incarceration in which the loss of everything and everyone familiar to them, physical suffering, weird noises, and fluorescent lights twenty-four hours a day rob them of their reason? And then, how medics in the ICUs add insult to injury, by dismissing the condition as ICU psychosis?

Would she not laugh bitterly at the paradox in which people have to protect themselves against the medical system by signing advance medical directives? 'But,' is she not likely to ask, 'If that generation knew the duty of care, why did the medical system decide to inflict that kind of pointless suffering on anyone? Why did it want every human being to protect oneself by creating legally binding documents?'

---

*Ibid.

I can almost see that researcher drawing in her breath in shock at the report that in 2015, more than 55 million Indians had been pushed below the poverty line due to out-of-pocket health expenditure.[*] What kind of healthcare was that, would she not wonder, that treated diseases and at the same time destroyed the health of whole families with catastrophic health expenditure!

That researcher is likely to marvel at how close we got to a solution. She would note how in 1948, the WHO defined 'health' as 'complete physical, mental, and social well-being and not merely the absence of disease or infirmity'.[**] She may look for evidence to show why this was ignored by the medical system but may not find much. But she may notice some changes in phrasing used by medical professionals and others in related fields—in the 1960s, they still talked about 'health-care service' but a while later, the term was abandoned in favour of 'healthcare industry'.

She may sit back and ponder whether this indicated a change in the way we thought and acted, whether the motivation to ease suffering gave way in our brave new industrialized world to an urge to consider human suffering as an opportunity to make profit. She may wonder whether we—an interesting syndicate of the pharma industry, equipment manufacturers, exporters, importers, politicians, bureaucrats, and doctors—started considering ourselves successful only if we could extract more and more profit out of human suffering!

---

[*]Selvaraj, Farooqui, and Karan, 'Quantifying the financial burden of households' out-of-pocket payments on medicines in India'.
[**]See www.who.int/about/governance/constitution.

She may be amazed by how a practical model to turn a cruel system into a compassionate care system—the palliative care movement—developed and proved itself to be viable in the twentieth century. She would note how Dame Cicely Saunders pioneered the hospice/palliative care movement and showed that medicine could still be humane. She would see how some doctors, nurses, and others—professionals and non-professionals—combined science with compassion in healthcare delivery and made lives liveable for people nearing the end of life. She would marvel at the resistance to change by the medical profession, how even after half a century, healthcare systems failed to adopt Saunders's model of care aiming at physical, social, mental, and spiritual well-being.

We, who are part of the healthcare system, have a choice. We can continue to be insensitive to human suffering and keep turning it all into profit for ourselves; but the backlash cannot be too far away. At the moment we are protected because we hold all the power and because those who are disease-stricken and their families are weak and powerless. But history tells us that no kind of oppression and exploitation can go on forever. We have the alternative of turning the system around and infusing compassion into it, changing it from a heartless industry to a vibrant combination of brain, heart, and hands.

You and I cannot shift the blame to governments and systems and escape our responsibility. When millions are in cruel, needless pain because we fail to adopt obvious and simple inexpensive solutions to the problem, the blame rests squarely on every healthy citizen in every democratic country.

If we choose to face the fact that the medical system has lost its sense of direction at least in part, then we can ask ourselves what we can do about it. Can we not integrate palliative care into all healthcare settings as recommended by the World Health Assembly in 2014 so as to relieve suffering along with treatment of diseases? Why can we not? Because palliative care is not expensive enough and so profit margins are lower?

When I talked about this choice to a group of doctors, a dear teacher-friend, Dr Michael Minton asked me, 'Raj, are you turning into a politician?'

I am grateful to him for asking that question. It made me think, and answer him with a quote by Donald Berwick: 'To try to avoid the political fray through silence is impossible, because silence is now political. Either engage or assist the harm. There is no third choice.'*

---

*Donald M. Berwick, 'Moral choices for today's physician', *JAMA*, Vol. 323, No. 17, 2020, pp. 2081–82.

FORTY-FIVE

CELEBRATING LIFE; CELEBRATING DEATH

Anatole Broyard, a former editor of the *New York Times* book review section, wrote, 'In learning to talk to his patients, the doctor may talk himself back into loving his work.... If he does, they (the patients) can share, as few others can, the wonder, terror and exaltation of being on the edge of being, between the natural and the supernatural.'[*]

How true! How absolutely true; even if you or I may not agree with everything that he wrote from his sickbed. We in palliative care have the unmatched privilege of working with people who allow us to see their lives in all their depth, sadness, and beauty. People who until then appeared to be ordinary, reveal to us their infinite strength, wisdom, and courage. They also let us in to lay bare their weaknesses and shortcomings and hold up a mirror to our shared frailty.

Blessed by this great privilege, I hope I have learnt enough from the people I have walked alongside for a while, to give me equanimity when I face my own death some day.

---

[*]Anatole Broyard, 'Doctor Talk to Me', *New York Times Magazine*, 26 August 1990.

If given a choice, I would like the time of my dying to be a time of celebration. If I get some time between a diagnosis and my death, and if the disease is incurable and not easily controlled, I would like my caring team to make me as comfortable as possible, so that I can spend the remaining time the way I want to.

I hope my family will accompany me on the path that I choose, and not drag me along in the direction that they decide on, even if they think there are certain miraculous solutions to be found there.

I hope the custodians and practitioners of the science I have learnt, the noble medical science, will be compassionate and remember that there is an art to healing as well. I hope they will not succumb to some inner Frankenstein, programmed to believe that they are obliged to keep my heart beating, or that a beating heart is more valuable than a peaceful existence; greater than the cost it inflicts on me and my loved ones. I fervently wish that I am not imprisoned in a cold intensive care room, isolated from my family when I need them the most. I hope my fellow health professionals will permit themselves to recognize that just as they have a duty to cure my disease if possible, they must also accept incurability when inevitable, and that just as they respect life, they need to respect death too.

I hope they will not shy away from the word 'dignity' and discard it as too unscientific simply because they do not have the tools with which to adequately measure it. I hope they will not make me spend hours on a trolley outside the radiology room to assess the progress of my disease, even when the results make little difference to my welfare. No therapeutic scan has yet been created that can measure happiness. There is no medical intervention yet that can generate joy, but the love that I give and the love I receive may be able to do that. If I am made physically comfortable within reasonable limits, this love could well be the only thing that matters as death approaches.

I believe that I, like every one of the estimated 7.8 billion human beings in this world, have a right to be treated by the medical system with the respect and dignity each one of us is entitled to, even when I am ill or dying, even when I no longer have the strength to fight for my rights. I believe I have a right to a compassionate and responsive medical system that will not reject the human being in me simply because my disease is incurable. I will consider it the greatest outrage on my person if, at that time, I am subjected to the ultimate indignity of a tube in every orifice, the agony of a suction catheter in my lungs, and the horror of a friendless, cable-covered, electronic inhumane death.

Some day, it is my hope that palliative care will be so well-integrated into medical practice that someone like me will not have to make this plea. I acknowledge that this is unlikely to happen in my lifetime, and so I am likely to need my friends in palliative care. I hope I am not force-fed if I am no longer hungry; I hope my doctor will not fear administering a sedative if I indicate that I want to sleep; I hope that if I reach out, my hand will be met with a friendly grasp in the darkness.

And even if ill, I may want to read once more, 'with tears, what her life with me has written upon her face'[*] and say a

---

[*]Kahlil Gibran, 'The Life of Love', *A Tear and a Smile*, available at <4umi.com/gibran/smile/16>.

final word of farewell to Chandrika, as Kahlil Gibran said. And to hold the hands of my children for a while and, with luck, to receive a final farewell kiss from my grandchildren.

But in the meantime, friends at Pallium India, while I am still very much here with you and not quite embracing the Grim Reaper just yet, maybe during a weekly team meeting let us have a small party to celebrate our lives together. Nothing elaborate—I fancy an 'ada' with the usual chai together and a bit of conversation. I want to be able to tell you how much you matter to me.

And to everyone who has given me abundant love, my family, and friends; those who arrived as patients and their families and became fellow travellers, teachers, and partners; my many colleagues past and present—there must have been so many ways in which I could have treated you better. I hope you will not find it too difficult to forgive me my faults and weaknesses. If you can think of a few good moments that you and I shared, my life has been worth living.

EPILOGUE

Many people have shared different parts of Dr Raj's journey with him. We have had the joy and honour of accompanying Dr Raj during a time when so much was in transition—within the inner circle that makes up Pallium India, the larger circle that includes our country brimming with new ideas and champions, and on the international level, as global dynamics and paradigms shift and realign to accommodate the truly massive purview of palliative care as an approach as much as a science.

The journey of palliative care in India has been a long, sometimes overwhelming, but rewarding one. While India's burden of health-related suffering is nowhere close to obliteration, palliative care has entered the nation's public health vocabulary in the last two decades. Many significant changes took place in this time. The Global South's first palliative care policy was formulated in Kerala; the draconian Narcotics, Drugs and Psychotropic Substances (NDPS) Act was amended, easing access to essential pain relief medicines for millions. The country also formulated a National Program for Palliative Care (NPPC) and has included palliative care in the service package being rolled out through Health and Wellness Centres (HWCs) nationwide. Pallium India has had the privilege of being a part of all these initiatives.

While all this tremendous progress has taken place, the reality remains that only a negligible proportion of both the common and the uncommon men, rich and poor alike, has access to appropriate palliative care. This is compounded by the fact that in the absence of strong social services, a larger number of people in countries like India need palliative care than in rich western nations.

There are champions scattered across the country, leading the charge and building on the achievements of our pioneers. They are to be found in private practice, touched by loss and grief, or moved and mobilized by the disparity and inequity they witness. There are the ones providing components of palliative care within public institutions, carving out a niche to somehow bring a palliative care approach to their practice even if creating a department is an uphill task. These champions often work against systemic barriers rather than being enabled by the system. The changes made at the policy level need to be translated into action to realize the goal of removing preventable suffering, mitigating suffering in chronic conditions, and offering care to the dying and those close to them.

The Kerala story has taught us that, as the Maori saying goes, it is always 'the people, the people, the people'; that the thread of policy change without handing controls back to the community will never become woven into the larger fabric of sustained change. The way forward for India is to bring people into the space of shared decision-making (public engagement), show them that appropriate and affordable care is a right, not charity (building awareness), and encourage them to speak up for themselves as much as we are there to bolster these invisible and unheard voices (demand for services), and for public and private providers to deliver services and be held accountable.

There is a whole generation of people who want to see a better, more accessible and equitable world, and they crowd the hallways of medical institutions in the millions. The soil is fertile for seeds of future leadership to be sown and the government can, if they wish, easily nurture them. For this to happen, appropriate content and time for palliative care has to be given its rightful place of priority in medical education. More people need to be enabled by the system to create models of care in their own settings, no matter how diverse or far flung, so that the glass ceiling of that one golden model can be gloriously shattered across the country.

Once people realize they have options against suffering, the word will spread, improving access and quality of services.

All of us will experience or witness serious health related suffering. Each of us will witness many deaths and one day our time will be up. We will all be carers or need care at some point. None of these need to be as painful as they currently are for most.

The solutions are known to us.

To paraphrase Neale Donald Walsch: let us seek them no longer, but now call them forth.

—Smriti Rana and Harsh Vardhan Sahni

ACKNOWLEDGEMENTS

My family who fuelled me with love.

Ms Gilly Burn and Dr Robert Twycross, my first gurus in palliative care.

Mr Gopal Krishna Pillai IAS, Mr Vijayachandran IAS, and Mr Venkatakrishnan.

The late Mr Bruce Davis and Ms Doreen Davis.

Dr M. C. Mehanathan, Mr P. V. Subba Rao, Mr Rajesh Nandan Srivastava, former directors of Narcotics, Department of Revenue, Government of India.

The late Mr Keshav Desiraju IAS, former Principal Secretary (Health), Government of India.

Mr S. M. Vijayanand IAS, former Chief Secretary, Kerala.

Dr Sudhir Gupta MD, additional director general of Health Services, Government of India.

Mr Harsh Vardhan Sahni, who wrote the epilogue with Ms Smriti Rana.

Ms Ann Felicity Westmore, Ms Smriti Rana, Ms Jeena Papaadi, Ms Kavitha Shanmugam, and Ms Sindhu S.

Ms Ashla Rani and Ms Deepa Srikumar for precious secretarial assistance.

Dr V. R. S. Nair, Mr Nandan, Dr Nirmala, and Dr C. Mohanan.

Mr Mike Hill and Ms Sue Collins for the movie *Hippocratic* (hippocraticfilm.com).

The numerous patients, their families, volunteers, colleagues, and healthcare professionals from whom I learnt valuable lessons.

CLOSING

Thank you for getting to this page. If this book has evoked any thoughts in you, please share them with me at mrraj47@gmail.com.

For example,

'My aunt suffers from.... How can I help her?'

'I want to initiate a palliative care service in.... Who can help me?'

'I liked what you wrote about...' or 'I disagree with you when you say....'

I promise a response.

Printed in Great Britain
by Amazon